Perfect Prey

Surviving a Cyber Shark's Romantic Fraud

Liz Cole

Manor House Publishing

Perfect Prey

**Library and Archives Canada
Cataloguing in Publication**

Cole, Liz / Perfect Prey
Surviving a Cyber Shark's Romantic Fraud

ISBN 978-1-897453-10-0

1. Title
2. First edition
3. Appendix

Published September 2009: Manor House Publishing

All rights reserved

Cover design/realization: Donovan Davie

Manor House Publishing Inc.
452 Cottingham Crescent, Ancaster, ON, :L9G 3V6
www.manor-house.biz
905-648-2193

Perfect Prey

Introduction

I live in an imperfect world with other imperfect people. I attract pain and disappointment. I cannot guarantee my own safety or ever be certain that I am in control of anything. My mind-sets, habits and feelings all combine to form a bull's eye. I was the target of a sociopath, a victim of a romantic fraud resulting from on-line dating; and now I am your wake-up call. My particular con artist has served time in federal and provincial prisons on at least ten occasions over the past 30 years and continues to fly under the radar of local law enforcement, most of the time. His crimes range from white-collar, corporate fraud; to personal scams and physical brutality against women. Many people close to me think I am out of my mind for even reporting this story. To them I say: If you know something must change, it is you that must make the change happen.

A romantic fraud occurs when a stranger simulates romantic intentions for the purpose of gaining affection and then using that goodwill to gain access to their victim's money, bank account or social connections to commit financial fraud. This is one of our society's dirty little secrets. The con artist achieves much of his or her wealth through consensual exchange making it difficult for authorities to link his or her conduct with crime. Sociopaths are often charismatic and charming. They are disorganized and lack the skills for maintaining normal behaviour. Unlike a psychopath, whose crimes are planned out, the sociopath is more likely to leave pockets of evidence in his or her explosions of violence or fraudulent conduct. It is their inability to feel remorse or guilt that makes my pursuit bittersweet. In addition to my story, other victims' stories are also told in the pages ahead. While not all are victims of *romantic* fraud they are victims of fraud. The actions of one man have permanently damaged many lives. His rampage stops with me, at least for a while.

My original purpose for recording the events of this past year was therapy. The first section is told as a narrative intended to help you understand the circumstances that led me into harm's way. The second section is written as a journal that describes the first 75 days in the company of the Irish Lad con artist. The third section, also a journal, describes the steps I have taken to regain my dignity by becoming active in the capture of this predator. Included in this section are several first person accounts from men and women across Canada who were defrauded by John Melvin Hill. This section will conclude with the actions effected by CTV's W-Five and me that resulted in the episode aired for Canadians on November 3 and 4, 2007. The balance of this book will combine the expertise of mental health professionals and organizations that specialize in romantic fraud and my own lessons learned.

Many of the names of central characters have been changed to protect personal identities. The names of my children and friends remain authentic. Further to the *authenticity* of my story is the risk of liability. The description of events regarding the failure of my marriage is representative of my experience of the truth. I am in part responsible for the demise of this marriage and accept my part. It was suggested I cite the reason for the end of my marriage as irreconcilable differences – so let's go with that. A disclaimer: We are not all seeking to harm one another. However, 1.89 million males and 1.95 million females considered sociopaths in North America *are* – and you need to know this. A sociopath disregards feelings and rights of others. They also disregard rules, social mores and laws and are unmindful of putting themselves or others at risk.

Part 1

Are you ready?

Can you hear me screaming? Can you see me crying? Do you taste the bile in my throat as I swallow the pain of being at the end of my own rope? Of course you can't. I wouldn't let you, until now.

This is my story.
It started out small, only one square foot. But as time marched on, the doormat I wove for the men in my life to walk on grew, slowly at first until finally I became wall-to-wall carpet. I don't even remember the runner or area rug phase. I just remember being on my hands and knees spot-cleaning the facts to protect my state of remaining unaware. Women know this lie. It is at the root of so many of our tragedies. It is the product of fear combined with ego to hold on to the status quo. But that's not all. The lie is large and is concealed by talking instead of listening. The lie keeps us in our comfort zone rather than being willing to risk. The lie helps us to pretend and prevents us from asking questions.

Fear of abandonment. Fear of rejection. Fear of conflict or confrontation. Fear of criticism. Fear of anger. Pick one. I own them all. It is even fair to say that I have operated with a certain pride of ownership.

And though pride goes before the fall, I gave my all for nothing in the end. I will even go as far to say I deserve nothing in the end. *GASP!* There I said it. I deserve nothing because I regarded myself as nothing. And though I ain't a math genius I do know that nothing from nothing leaves nothing. I sold me out. I spent well over 15 years curbing my anger, laughing in the face of sadness and working hard not to offend others. I sacrificed joy.

This is not a tale of self-pity. It is a wake-up call for anyone who negotiates their self-worth as badly as I have. Raised right, educated, loved and nurtured, I still messed up. I was afraid to inconvenience my mental health and get some help dealing with any of my fears. Don't get me wrong, I didn't just wake up with this anxiety ridden shopping list. I had earned them. At first by a Father who abandoned me to play house with a replacement family and second by a Husband who regarded my worth as follows: "When you make as much money as I do, then you will be in a position to ask me to do something for you."

I have no plans of making this story about either my Father or my ex-Husband. I only introduce them to you because of what happens next in my life. About my Dad, I want you to know that I adored him. His quiet strength and affection guided me well into my adolescence and for that I will always love him. My resignation to his rejection will never be entirely complete. I do recognize that I did not choose my Father, rather his sperm chose my Mother's egg and the rest is biology.

My ex-Husband is not going to get off as gracefully. That was his choice, not mine, and this is why: On June

14, 2005, my Husband of 22 years decided to "reduce" his life by three people. He announced he was leaving me, and effectively, our daughters as well.

As if it could not get any worse, his announcement came on the afternoon following our daughter's Grade Eight Graduation. Still basking in the afterglow from the awards delivered to both daughters, my Husband managed to levy the one-two punch minutes before the children walked through the door, and as with most special occasions, the plan was to have a dinner celebration. Well, dinner hour came and went without me. I could barely breathe much less swallow. His employment ended on June 10th with a major mutual fund company, leaving him jobless.

So let's recap: Within one week my Husband had lost his job and quit our marriage.

My Husband had worked for a mutual fund company for the better part of 14 years as a mainframe computer consultant. He was excellent at this job and well regarded by his peers. His compensation was generous, and our lifestyle reflected his earning capacity. He loved to spread his wealth around Yorkville, a posh neighbourhood frequented by celebrities and beautiful people. One bar in particular, Hemingways, benefited handsomely from his good fortune. The servers and barmaids benefited from the many, many long nights and weekends he put in at the bar. Oops, I meant to say working late at the office.

His way of being fair was to provide our daughters with expensive clothing, tickets to ball games, cash flow and a doormat for a wife who would manage their every need in his never ending absence. Don't get me wrong, sometimes I was invited to attend a ball game.

The writing was on the wall for his future as a consultant. As far back as Christmas 2004, he knew that his days were numbered. Still he did nothing. In the days before his contract ended on June 10, 2005, a client offered him a full-time position with stock options, benefits and a fair living wage. He declined favouring his market worth elsewhere. He did so knowing that I only worked part-time, a mutual decision that allowed me to raise our daughters. He did so knowing our debt ratio. He did so knowing he planned to abandon us.

Where do you sleep the first night after you are told that you do not matter?

Strangely, my reaction was to stand in front of a mirror and take stock. Not a full-length mirror mind you as that was simply a source of too much information. Rather, I stood mid-drift upward and examined my rather unexamined life. I am 42 years old, 15 pounds overweight, have no money of my own in the bank, and have two children who hang on my every word, decision and facial expression.

How do you keep your game face on to protect your children? *Why didn't you devote more time to amassing personal financial security? How will this end?* And, what, if anything, did the past 22 years mean? Perhaps most importantly, who do you tell this information to first?

Let me answer the last question first. I called my family doctor. Not a lawyer. Not my Mother, a business associate or best friend. Why? Because I was able to anticipate the pain and disruption for my children down the road.

The Doctor set up a care plan that would have them attend counselling at North York General Hospital's Paediatric Psychiatric Department. They would guide, support, listen too and empower my daughters. The team's social worker, by far the most influential member of the team, gave my daughters a chance to process their pain and move beyond it toward a reasonably normal and bright future.

Now it's your turn to scream

I did not retain a lawyer until the winter of 2006. I was not in a coma, just overwhelmed by my reality. It was a huge mistake that has cost me every last cent. Living in a dream world believing my Husband would never neglect his children. I confused emotion with the business of divorce. There is no room for sentimentality at this table. Allowing him this head start gave him the chance to establish a home court advantage from sunny California. This misstep has cost me tens of thousands of dollars and will continue to cost me a great deal of money because I know the law protects the clients with the largest retainer. I am telling you this because it is a textbook example of how off kilter my radar was.

You can only flush one toilet at a time

I kept the secret of my abandonment from my Mom. My shame, disillusionment, and lack of choices choked me from uttering the words: "Mom I'm in trouble and need to move home with the girls." Instead, I packed up the van and took the girls camping, as planned for several weeks. Not only did I pack the van, but I packed

240 pounds of confusion. You see, when my Husband gave me the boot, I offered him an escape clause. I suggested that he use the period of July 1st through July 19th to weigh his decision. In effect I gave him the luxury of remaining in control of my future, stationed comfortably in our beautiful home while I assumed responsibility for the girls in Killbear Provincial Park.

Camping is great for people who need to step outside their connected lives. It is like being alone in a dark sensory deprivation chamber with only your thoughts and imagination to keep you from going insane. But what happens when you already are temporarily insane?

Well in my case, I read a book a day, drank a bottle of wine a day, walked five miles a day, and mostly stared off into the vastness of the Georgian Bay. My dear friend, Suki, was at my side the entire time and allowed me to have my breakdown in silence. Other friends, Liz and Michael and their girls, joined us for a couple of days just to keep an eye on me.

I wanted to scream, I needed to scream. I wanted to cry, I needed to cry. Instead I sucked it up. Liar.

On July 19th I made a b-line for my Husband who remained in our family home back in Toronto. I had planned to stay up North until the 20th but our site became swarmed with bees. Getting stung was not an option. Going home and getting eaten alive was.

With the roar of the laundry machines in the background of our basement, I asked my Husband if he had changed his mind and wanted to work on our marriage. I could hear myself say the words, but I knew that it was over. I guess I thought this gesture of maturity displayed grace under fire. Who the hell cared, nobody was watching. He responded with a dismissive, cutting remark that he found looking at me made him ill.

Why would he say such a vile thing? He already had his freedom dangling within reach. I suppose it was to affirm his decision to make a run for it. After all, what person would chase after someone following a comment like that?

Five loads of laundry later, I was in the car, heading for my Mom's house, alone. I needed to confess my reality and rally support. The children remained home for the next few hours spending quality time with their Father.

As I drove away from our home I uttered the words "dream house." It was behind me now. A fully updated ranch style bungalow with large principal rooms, multiple bathrooms, landscaped property, and walls painted in colours such as sun-dried tomato and herbs de Provence. The main bedroom paint was called Sunday morning. This was not a dream house, it was purgatory.

Six short driving minutes away awaited Mom's precious 800-square-foot semi-detached bungalow, which has two bedrooms and one bathroom. Delicate is an understatement. Antique plate rails, pink floral everything and scented candles flood the senses on arrival. Located in the middle of the block on a street in Leaside, a community in Toronto where nothing bad ever happens. That's what any Leasider will tell you. The neighbours combine to form the world's longest freestanding hug. This house is bigger than a bread box. Was it big enough for all of us? It had to be.

Mom had no idea that any of this chaos had taken place. With Mom's driveway only feet away, my stomach went into spasm and my head began pounding. I was about to tell my Mommy that my Husband of 22 years wanted out of our marriage and had not been successful finding work. However, his golf game had picked up.

I walked through Mom's door, sat down on her doll-sized love seat and said the words, "it's over." I cried, only for a second or two. Really. I felt shame, rage and panic all at once and there just wasn't space left for tears. Naturally Mom asked why? I told her how he found me to be disgusting and that the only thing wrong with his life was the fact that I was part of it. Mom knew that he had quite a history as a barfly. She was nobody's fool and had kept tabs on the number of nights I spent alone in every one of our homes. At various points along the way I shared greeting cards sent to him from other women. Then there were the phone calls from waitresses from various restaurants such as Mother Tuckers', Hooters, you know, quality establishments. Not the kind of calls that said, "please tell your Husband he has left his sunglasses, or wallet or balls." Just giggling stupid calls that chirped, "tell him I called and will see him soon."

In the blink of an eye

My Mother took a deep breath, possibly her last and told me to go home and get my children. I nodded knowing this was it. Days away from turning 43 and I was moving home to my Mom's house. Everything I had worked for, lived for and loved for was yesterday's news. With what little sanity I could muster, I suggested that the move could be postponed as I would prefer to spend the balance of the summer at our home in Collingwood. Secretly I was hoping for the divine hand of God to reach down and stop my life from speeding out of control.

You may be wondering why on earth the children and I would leave our home rather than ask him to leave. He didn't even offer. The clock was ticking as there was a big mortgage and no income. It was only a matter of weeks before we would have to list the house for sale anyway. Besides I was not the kind of person to make demands. I had a history of being walked on to protect.

He did suggest that we could all continue to live under one roof meantime. If that happened, I would have murdered him and the balance of this story would have been written as a prison journal.

Collingwood Condominium: Last Marital Asset

The Girls and I spent the balance of the summer at our condominium in Collingwood. With my Mom at my side, I wandered around in a fog. She began shifting her mind-set and square footage to welcome us home. As well as opening her heart and front door to the three of us, our package also came with a dog.

My daughters and our dog, Kobe moved home to the little old china shop the weekend following Labour Day. It was my worst fear that Rachel's teacher would ask her to write a brief essay on *What I did on my summer vacation.*

The plan was to catch our breath and with the help of my Husband's financial support, be out of my mom's house within six months. Who was I kidding?

A Labour of Love

We moved into Mom's house following Labour Day Weekend. It was my intention to create instant normalcy. The girls would have access to all their clothing, technology and lip gloss. I would live on the head of a pin and remain silent, living only inside my head.

My Husband seemed numb to his reality. No income, no employment prospects, no interest in spending time with his children; but still a mighty fine golf game. I went to the marital home and stated the house must go up for sale immediately. Had he experienced a full-blown mid-life crisis and was now realizing the impact of his actions? For the first time, his $5,000 Calloway Golf Clubs may be without a home. The new Durango with heated seats, without a driveway, need I go on? Did I care? Too busy, too broke, and too exhausted. It was time to contact the Millar Team, our real estate professionals and loosen the noose around our neck.

I think listing the house was the final nail in my coffin. I had been working on raw energy since June 14th – actually for years. It was a Wednesday morning, mid-September. I woke up. I made lunches. I dressed for an important client meeting. I walked the dog. I came through the front door, fainted and then threw up.

I missed the meeting.

The look of horror on Rachel's face said it all. Our new reality had finally exploded. Mom and Rachel helped to undress me and place me in Mom's bed. With a cold compress on my forehead and a plastic-lined wastebasket at my side, I managed to call my business partner and tell her she was flying solo.

I was ill again, and again for the balance of the day. With nothing left to lose I clutched my pillow in search of hope and dignity. I found neither. I slept for 18 hours. I awoke Thursday morning and vowed never to lose one more day.

Fantasy Island

My Husband had no immediate plans to re-engage with work and spent some of this downtime packing for the upcoming moving day. Our house had now sold. The closing date was November 4, 2005.

November 4th went as smoothly as could be expected. Mid-afternoon, the house was clean and ready to receive the new family.

My Husband drove to our home in Collingwood. He remained there until mid-March of the following year. The condominium unit is 1,219 square feet of updated living space featuring three bedrooms, three bathrooms, and no property management responsibilities. He would, however, visit Toronto once a week to spend about an hour with his daughters over dinner at a local pub.

Go West Midlife Crisis Man

Sometime during the second week of March 2006, my Husband returned to Toronto. Only flying through town, he called and suggested that we have a family dinner at Mom's house. He'd pick up some chicken and chips to set the stage for his "announcement." With precious moments to spare, I shuffled Mom down the block to our friend Kerry's house. Having Mom on deck would have resulted in the kind of confrontation that I have dreaded my entire life. With Mom out the door, I knew that Toronto would have one less homicide victim.

Minutes into the dipping sauce, he announced that he accepted a short-term six-month contract in Salinas, California. He was leaving within the next four days.

With dinner behind us, I asked our daughters to give me a moment to speak with their Dad. We needed to talk about money. Specifically *his* money and how we would be receiving it. He was sweet and sympathetic as he checked his watch and fished for his car keys.

He had no plans for our future, and no thoughts about childcare. It was his opinion that my Mother should take us in, expenses and all. He told me the children and I had a good ride and it was over.

I called a lawyer. He already had a lawyer, whom I'll herewith refer to as Lawzilla.

Mr. $375 an Hour was recommended to me for his deliberate rational way. This lawyer was not about theatrics. He was about process and logic.

In my usual polite, non-confrontational way, Mr. $375 an Hour and I had our first meeting. I glossed over the harshness of my reality and went as far to suggest the terms of my separation agreement and subsequent divorce would prove rather unremarkable. This first meeting marked the beginning of a lengthy and costly relationship.

If a tree falls in the forest and nobody is there to hear it does it make a sound? Yes. The sound is coming from a nearby paper mill keeping up with the paper demands for the unrelenting documentation proving that you do in fact buy groceries, pay utility bills, and pick up the occasional expense associated with your daughters' dance classes.

The apparent strategy for Lawzilla's team was to tie me up via the producing of mind numbing financial documentation. This would serve to exhaust my time and money. I could not afford to lob the ball back over the net as many times nor would I because I dislike confrontation. I was a doormat during our marriage and our divorce.

Divorce is not funny

During my marriage, I learned a great deal about myself. In particular how to lie down, play dead, get back up, make dinner, lather, rinse and repeat.

I buried simple truths to protect myself from pain. For the record, simple truths usually weigh ten pounds, are maple or caramel flavoured and rest comfortably on your ass. Burial on the other hand always involves drinking much wine. I've rationalized my dramatic increase in wine consumption by recognizing the death of my marriage as an occasion for hosting a private wake.

After a year of licking my wounds, still failing to let them heal, I became intrigued by the prospect of blind-dating. Blind-dating does not afford you the luxury of dulled reality. It needs you to have Spidey-like senses, witty comebacks, patience and flavoured lip-gloss. It forces you to upgrade your appearance and upload new intelligence. Who you were no longer matters when hunting for new love. Who you are while on the date is under review.

The upside to blind dating in your 40's is that you have arrived at the altar of middle-age. On a good day you are not sporting new hairs on your breasts and your abdomen is not bloated beyond next Tuesday. I'd be lax if I overlooked the natural beauty of a man with a great benefit package and vested pension. Mom always said, "It's just as easy to love a rich man as a poor man."

One short year after my marriage ended, I realized that I must have believed that having a bad marriage was better than being alone. I'd lost sight of my reality. I was and will always be an extraordinary woman, as are all women. Like so many women, I was at high-risk for entering destructive relationships. You know, the easy relationships based on high percentages of jerks, players and just plain dangerously wrong guys. Extraordinary does not necessarily mean being self-aware. Simple questions needed to be asked – if not by myself, then by others who could have stopped me. Questions like: Are you lonely? Do you have a strong self-esteem? Do you consider yourself to be streetwise? Are you financially stable? These questions are among many that could have saved me from me.

Juggling my ignorance about the world that awaited me with the cruelty of my Husband and his lawyer made it impossible for me to see straight. No free time, no money, and no hope combined to wear me down and feel even worse about myself.

If there was to be a man in my future he had to want to be in the presence of a woman who gave 100% and was not intimidated by that.

I want to be the life partner that anticipates the needs and wants of her loved ones and then makes a reasonable effort to deliver them. I want to create a living space for family to feel safe and open to relax.

I guess that makes me a freak.

Somewhere between a rock and a hard place, I sidestepped getting my emotional house in order and began the search for companionship. It was May 2006, the season of Liz. It was time to spring forward. My travelling companions: loneliness, insecurity, inexperience and poverty were at my side nicely packaged in trust, ambition and devotion to motherhood.

Now you know me.

Magical thoughts.

Before attracting a date I secretly harbour magical thoughts. I blame them on Walt Disney characters and any movies with Meg Ryan and Tom Hanks. In truth, I want a 50-something, long-time divorced or widowed man with well-adjusted children, who happens to practice family law and has a reputation for being ruthless in the courtroom. In his private life he finds time to walk orphaned puppies.

Magical thoughts are not necessarily productive and often need a prescription.

Is there anyone out there?

Seriously, is there anybody out there that does not fit one of the following descriptions?
- Still married. Not divorced for reasons that only make sense to the pocketbook.
- Seeing other people as well as you.
- Coping with past pain while seeking new pain.
- Still lives with parents.
- A sociopath.

When you begin the hunt all bright eyed and bushy tailed your delusion serves and protects. You can't remember the horror of dating from decades ago much like you can't recall the pain of childbirth.

I become the hunter

The hunter spends hours in preparation. You are keenly aware about the rules of first impression. There is a checklist that includes the outer trappings of a projected self-confidence, perfect hair and make-up, flattering undergarments, cash in your wallet and a fully charged cell phone. The inner checklist reminds you to shave above the knee. Minty fresh breath is implied. Oh yes, the mantra: "Don't drink too much. Don't drink too much. Don't drink too much. Take a cab."

Summertime is a tad trickier in that you must incorporate the pedicure. Why? I don't know, because getting naked can happen in any season.

Mating season has begun

Blinded by my enthusiasm, I did not know that dating was something you did to find out whether you

Perfect Prey

wanted to get involved or just window-shop. I believed that if you hit it off on the first and second dates you were, therefore, a couple. Taking my time was and is foreign. You should see how fast I eat.

First, you advertise your availability. Everyone knows someone who has a brother, uncle, co-worker, rehab buddy or parole officer. Second, you describe your level of enthusiasm to have sex. This creates a sense of urgency that helps keep things moving forward.

Fortunately, this is not an advice book on how to date. Nor is this a book about my blind-dating rampage. Rather, this is the back story that led me into harm's way.

A wonderful woman who worked at one my client sites suggested an intimate dinner party at her home featuring her out-of-town brother, a social worker. Perfect. Trained to listen, experienced in the ways of spotting a variety of mental health disorders and most importantly, has a pulse.

I dated Mr. Social Worker for two months and would describe my emotional state as highly caffeinated. This man is a "good guy." He has a sensible lifestyle, recognizes the importance of being attracted to women that mirror his own values and interests, seeks equality in partnership, is supportive and well intentioned. How did I let this one get away? Simple, I forgot to clean my own emotional house before entertaining new guests.

Still in denial about my own state of mind, I ushered in round two. My daughter Rachel with the help of her best friend connected the dots between me and her uncle. Wasting no time at all, I went straight from the frying pan into the fire. As if possessed, I leapt into his volcano. Uncle Blind Date is 50, divorced and has no children. He already had a friendship with Rachel. He is masculine, musical, and harbours just the right amount of self-torturing angst. He has a hot-tub and a pool. I remained wet for two months. The volcano had to blow. We ended days before I made it to court in October. I was alone again.

Later in November, I had the most refreshing blind date imaginable. It was two hours long and took place in the lounge at the Keg Restaurant. On arrival, I noted him to be an attractive and welcoming man. We found our way to a table, ordered drinks and made small talk. His small talk changed my life. Seated before me was a mid 40s professional male who lives with his parents and always has. In his own words, he was "the glue that kept their 50 plus year marriage together." Enough said.

Later that night and in a weak moment…

I pulled out my Mastercard, fired up the laptop computer and enrolled for a three-month trial period on www.date.ca.

The personal profile application was intense. First, you itemize your appearance, followed by personal preferences, pet peeves, ideal date circumstances, outlook for the future of the world, recommendations for curing cancer and what your plan is to reduce the threat of global warming.

But the application *doesn't* ask if you have a criminal record or are known to the authorities. It also doesn't ask for any relevant information that could serve to flag you or your intended. I uploaded my life complete with photo and received 34 interested responses within 24 hours.

Perfect Prey

Blind Dating: The Other White Meat

To steal a line from one of my favourite movies, Highlander, "there can only be one." If I were to make my own movie, I would change this line to: "There can only be one at a time – or can there?" So, I picked one, but did I pick the right one?

We briefly e-mailed, he called, and we agreed to have lunch.

Lunch is the perfect time for a first date. It offers the built in excuse of having to return to work. I was on a real blind date flying blind without a safety net. He was a stranger, as was I to him. His profile was sufficiently interesting to warrant my attention and featured two key descriptions: divorced and non-smoker. I selected a local eatery named Fate Bistro. Close enough to my home to make a run for it and far enough away to make it a walk to remember.

I met Mr. Date.Ca and he was to my delight just as his photo and profile communicated minus the non-smoker part. This was a choice point. Do I anchor my response on this misinformation and determine he has lied to attract a wider audience? Do I suspend judgment and find empathy for this person battling an addiction? Instead I ordered a California salad with chicken, and a glass of Chardonnay. There was eye contact, hand touching, laughter and plenty of relaxation to swallow every bite of lunch.

Mr. Date.Ca helped me with my coat and then untucked my hair, allowing it to rest on the outside the collar. He suggested a walk, linked my arm to his, and we began our stroll complete with a pit stop to gawk at my precious minivan. We ended our walk with a brief sit down on a stone ledge outside the restaurant. The wind had tossed my hair and left a few curled strands falling before my left eye. Again, Mr. Date.Ca gently stroked away the strands, placed his palm on my face, and I knew at that moment that I welcomed a next date. We exchanged business cards and spoke of a next time. He asked me what I like to do on dates and I responded comedy clubs. Face-to-face we hugged, then kissed, then hugged. His fragrance was Polo Black. My expectation was that he would call again. He did not call. He did not e-mail. Too bad though because I liked this man. The hunt continues.

Later that same week, while serving a client, I managed to blurt out to my friends in law enforcement that they needed to find me a date. Just 24 hours later the e-mail arrived from the "date." Mr. Law and Order telephoned suggesting we go out on a date. Our conversation revealed that we attended the same high school during the same time-frame, yet our paths never crossed. We agreed to meet at a Tim Horton's Donut Shop to accomplish the "meet and greet" requirement. We agreed to proceed to dinner.

He was handsome and punctual, sporting a beautiful black leather coat and good fitting jeans. I couldn't help but imagine him in uniform. He made respectful references about his teenaged children and ex-wife. Even his coworkers noted him as a good guy.

Both my daughters understand that I want a social life. They are not looking for a replacement father; they just want me to get a life so that I will pay less attention to their lives. My older daughter struggles less with my choice of blind dates and more with how I appear on blind dates. She will offer moral support by asking: "What's this loser like?" Or, "Do you own any attractive clothes?" The benefit of having her around the house is that she helps you weed out undesirable clothing, which in my case is all my clothing. She has referred to me as appearing homeless. Ironically, I am.

My younger daughter's rules for dating the blind can be summed up in one sentence: money talks and ugly walks. However, there are exceptions to this rule and they are:

If he is younger by five or more years he must be both rich and hot.
If he is older by five or more years he must be rich because it's too late to be hot.
If he is about the same age then he needs to be reasonably good-looking and at least drive a cool car.

In the weeks following my first date with Mr. Law and Order a seed of doubt was planted by his colleague implying that I should expect Mr. Law and Order to be dating a host of other people because that's the way dating works. Translation: Dating more than one person at the same time is okay.

I am a consecutive dater. Should I be a concurrent dater? Mr. Law and Order is a great place to start. But in order to be a concurrent dater, you need at least two people to date at one time. So, I e-mailed Mr. Date.Ca and asked him if he had fallen off the planet. He quickly replied with a genuine apology suggesting that he didn't think I was interested in a second date and then followed up with a telephone call. There was definite interest to resume our friendship.

Perfect Prey

Mr. Date.Ca and I agreed to meet at an Italian eatery on Monday, December 11, 2006 at 7:00 P.M. He is best described as a warm blanket. Being near him feels like being tucked away for winter. Dinner was magnificent featuring an exciting menu and wine selection. I am allergic to garlic, and Mr. Date.Ca had taken the time to speak to restaurant staff, earlier in the day, to confirm that I had a significant number of safe selections available. He reserved a booth so we could sit side by side. I remember eating and drinking because that's what you do in restaurants. I will never forget kissing between bites.

Dinner was over by 9:00 P.M. Sure it was a school night, but I'd completed my homework. We were over 40 and wanted a little privacy. Mr. Date.Ca thinks well on his feet and suggested we visit his office, which was less than five minutes away. Imagine an entire office building with no obvious sign of cleaning staff?

We made our way to the boardroom and were able to table important agenda items. The meeting closed with an action item that affirmed our need to have the next meeting off-site.

I am cautious to suspend other dating interests because I am reminded of Mr. Law and Order's sage wisdom about dating and the need to keep it casual.

Mr. Date.Ca and I went on a field trip complete with a picnic lunch, just blocks away from Black Creek Pioneer Village. This was my very first encounter spending any time with any man in a rented room. It was nice to not have to make the bed. It was curious that we did not have our time together in his house given the children would have been in school.

Mr. Law and Order is off the radar. His social commitments, family duties and total inflexibility to rank me among his priorities, make him missing in action. Mr. Date.Ca continues to appear interested in me and offers just the right range of sentimentality, affection and elbow grease.

Christmas is Almost Here

The holidays magnify all things great and small. Magical thoughts are rapid firing. I envision Mr. Date.Ca attending our Christmas Eve open house and sneaking kisses under the mistletoe. He declined. Too busy, too complicated, too soon to meet his children ... too married? I had a hunch about the last one. Never mind, I had the spirit of the season and would take another run at him for New Year's Eve.

Dating after divorce is strange. It may be legitimate and perfectly natural, but I can't get over the feeling that I am the "other woman" in both my dates' lives. What is strange to me is how e-mailing and instant messaging have become the medium for most communication and the Internet a source for finding dates. The speed of e-mailing and instant messaging has us confusing information with intimacy. Feelings represent our true story, and an e-mail will never convey our true self. Steamy phrasing will never replace eye-contact. Still, Baby Boomers like me find ourselves over 23 million strong in the search for love on-line in North America.

It was already December 28th and I had yet to be asked out for New Year's Eve by either Mr. Law and Order or Mr. Date.Ca. Dating either of these men is testing my resolve. They didn't know me well enough to even know I have resolve. They didn't know that I would have given anything to be with Mr. Honey I'm Home.

Mr. Law and Order signed on to let me know that he might have a couple of minutes to grab a quick coffee New Year's Eve morning; a quick *45-minute* drive from my home. I declined. I asked him about his time over the next few days, and he quickly responded how the next several days were earmarked for family and friends. I replied: "Am I not counted among your friends?" No answer. Maybe he's just not that into me. Maybe this is casual dating.

Where the hell is Mr. Date.Ca?

It was 4:10 PM on December 28th and I decided to send one last e-mail in the hope of gaining his attention. I shut down the computer and joined the land of the living. I spent time with friends, eating, laughing and forgetting the time wasted these past few days on men. This turned out to be a great evening. I needed this evening.

Once home, I fired up the computer. A simple apology is offered from Mr. Date.Ca citing strep throat as the cause for delay. I liked Mr. Date.Ca and I wanted to be near him. We barely knew each other and I didn't even have his home address. I hadn't asked because I didn't want to confirm what I'd already suspected.

Do not be fooled by my exploits. Dating is not for the faint of heart. You need to develop a real toughness, an outer shell that protects you from the unavoidable rejection. The alternative is to stop all together and learn to knit or adopt cats – lots of cats.

Paul, a neighbour and friend currently working on his own writing project, asked me out to lunch. Among the many points of conversation about relationships he asked me if I had ever consciously selected a date based on similarities. Conversely, he asked me to identify the one date that was most fatal from the outset. I'm thinking: Pretty heavy chit-chat for a glass of wine and a grilled cheese – particularly since I had never done the homework.

Well knock me over with a feather!

Mr. Law and Order just called to conduct a spot check. He had no intentions of making plans; just wanted to check in to make certain that I am still hanging on to the possibility of even being interested in him. And so goes the pattern. Once again, "keep it moving, nothing to look at here."

It's official, I hate dating. I hate that the court allows my Husband to screw us. I hate spending every cent I earn on debt associated with his great escape.

I am beginning to hate everything. By God, I have finally allowed anger to find its way home.

I logged onto www.date.ca in the hope that Mr. Date.Ca wrote me a long, loving note that is largely intended to reassure me of his affections. Instead, I found I'd been "hot listed" by two complete strangers, nice enough in their own right, but I'm not interested.

Why on Earth is New Year's Eve such a bloody big deal for me? Normally I wouldn't place this day on such a high pedestal. I guess it is because my friends and family know I am dating. Even my Mom sought an update about New Year's Eve. I imagine that she was wondering about the kind of men I am attracting. Good question. What men am I attracting?

The Law of Attraction states that you attract the people and experiences you want consciously and unconsciously.

Despite the "tough talk" I would have melted if Mr. Date.Ca called and asked me out. My New Year's Resolution is clear; work on the Law of Attraction by clarifying your priorities. Clean up your inner house.

Based on the inbound online dating requests it would appear that I could easily attract significantly older, financially settled men. I am not bragging. My small business is not creating sufficient wealth to support my children and my Husband's deadbeat ways. I am scared to death. I am tired of losing and being forced to make all the necessary adjustments. I want one moment where it all works out.

Already December 30th and I wished that I would just disappear. Rachel was in Florida eagerly anticipating the celebration of her 13th birthday while Tess prepared for departure to Florida on the 2nd of January. I have financed these excursions by exhausting my line of credit. The Ex was supposed to forward money for the children but has yet to do so. I had to borrow from my Mom, *again*. Their Father has over 200,000 Air Canada Aeroplan Miles. Hmmm?

New Year's Eve happened without Mr. Date.Ca. I celebrated the end of the year with my own family and wonderful friends. I still didn't know where he lived, his phone number, or whether or not he is actually married, much less living with his spouse.

2007/Day One

I vowed to do things differently. I prayed to God for the strength to do things differently. I had been a passenger for most of my life and allowed the drivers to run me off the road.

Mom continued to remind me to create a little distance between me and my men. There was no mystery. I was an open book. She insisted that if I just sat back and resisted the urge to reach out and touch someone then maybe they would work a little harder to find me. She was right. It's just that I have romantic attention deficit disorder.

The Heart Wants What the Heart Wants...

My close friend and neighbour, Sarah called to wish me a Happy New Year. Her timing is always perfect. Sarah and I went for a walkie talkie. Thank God for Sarah. Together we are quite a force of nature. Apart we are effective and slightly fragile and must be handled with care.

Mr. Date.Ca e-mailed me to wish me a Happy New Year, and report that his own evening out was quiet and that he was busy all day today. In fact, he was busy all week as it is a short week. My reaction was pure rejection. Start fresh Liz. Walk away...

All in the name of research!

I had spent well over two hours surfing the Net for earth-shattering revelations about how not to sabotage new relationships with men. I came to the conclusion that the worst thing any woman can do is not be herself. The only way to attract someone and continue a relationship is to be comfortable with your own company. This was a problem for me: I was not enamoured with Liz Cole. She was tired, hurt, afraid, broke, and hard on herself.

One more thing…

All the dating and relationship experts stated that you should not confuse lust with love nor should you jump into sex too quickly. Understanding is one thing, acting is another. Sexual chemistry matters. Not just to me, but to most people. I need to experience a certain degree of satisfaction; it's basic to my contentment. Women are not encouraged to speak this truth. I did surf www.date.ca for new suitors and spotted a few eligible candidates. It was time to move forward. Mr. Date.Ca and Mr. Law and Order knew where to find me, let's just see how hard they'd try.

The past 18 months have been hell on me, on everyone. I tried to keep my fears and frustrations close to the vest. I needed a strong Father-figure in the fight against weapons of teenage destruction. Their actual Father was unavailable, golfing, deep sea fishing and learning to sky dive in California. My Mother had become the other parent and that was not right. She was the grandmother, the special person that your children threaten to run away to when their own parents mess up. Something had to give.

Mr. Date.Ca called to confirm his unavailability for the weekend. But as a compromise, he suggested an 'offsite' meeting between noon and 3 P.M. on Friday.

Perfect Prey

This time I made it work for me and made plans to continue on to Collingwood.

Mr. $375.00 an Hour called me to let me know the Ex's lawyer had opposed my motion for severing the marriage filed in October 2006. This should have been a done deal. His grounds were hollow, but sufficient enough to force a costly delay. My not-so ex-Husband had succeeded in bankrupting my spirit, time and money...

I managed to book a doctor's appointment to revisit existing prescriptions and acquire new ones.

I doubled the dose of my anti-depressants and recommitted to taking the birth control pill. In the course of conversation, I heard myself tell the Doctor that I needed to prevent unwanted pregnancy because I was dating a man that I met on the Internet.

Fortunately, I did not say that I do not know where the man I was dating lives, his home phone number or whether or not he was married or lives with his wife. I am surprised the Doctor didn't prescribe some form of anti-psychotic medication.

Once home from the doctor's office, I managed to partner with Sarah for another walkie talkie. This one required a Starbucks chaser. I told her that for the first time in six months I felt different about dating.

Sarah describes this as "the manic recovery period." By God, she nailed it. I have been out of control with my emotions.

Battle stations

It was Friday, January 12, 2007. Mr. $375.00 an Hour and I were in for a marathon appointment to sign off on various motions to be filed in Court. I was in debt for $42,000. I was supposed to be divorced. I was drowning.

My business continued to move at a snail's pace. I had given myself until the end of January to turn the Titanic around. My business partner, Susan, was aware of this and had committed to roll up her sleeves.

The time had come to shift gears. Do things differently. Try something new. I called the hairdresser and got bangs. I also invited Mr. Date.Ca to dinner on January 20th.

The book **What Smart Women Know** (by Steven Carter and Julia Sokol), tells women to never play house, much less cook a meal for your man unless you are in fact sharing that house. I have already admitted to handing out Christmas shortbread cookies and homemade soup, and now I have sent an invitation for Mr. Date.Ca to join me for dinner. I had failed womankind. I was about to be failed by the Ontario Family Court System.

Word from my lawyer confirmed that Thursday, January 25, at 10 A.M. was go-time. My Husband's lawyer planned to go after court costs for being rushed to appear. As for their claim of being rushed, our marriage ended on June 14, 2005, and it was now January 2007.

I had fully disclosed every last tedious financial document. I was, to date, the only caregiver and provider to our children. My Husband had managed to defer any requirement to produce financial disclosures, and was well on his way to securing another deferral. With great angst, Lawzilla pleaded for more time to review my financial documentation as her grounds for deferral. She also demanded a day of questioning in the presence of a court reporter.

We complied. We always comply.

It costs a lot of money to get the attention of a judge to rule in favour of children's rights. I had to decide whether to pay more money to my lawyer or feed my children.

I had become painfully aware that my mind had experienced noticeable wear and tear. I had lost the ability to be still, be direct and speak simple truths. Making eye contact was almost impossible. The damage to my psyche was so significant that I resorted to my natural wit and clever asides to keep from being truly recognized. I had amnesia in that I no longer recognized myself. My spirit was dead. I had thoughts of wishing I was dead too. I had convinced myself that I had made a real mess of things.

Be patient. Take your time. Time is money. Find the strength to go on.

Mom was weeks away from having a full knee replacement surgery on her right knee. The young orthopedic caring for Mom greeted us all bright-eyed with designer frames. I knew instantly that Mom was calculating his probable age and the price of his shoes. Going over the pros and cons for surgery, we could not help but notice his keen sense of fashion. The effortless way he matched chocolate brown and pale blue was a home run. His eye for mixing and matching guaranteed he'd select just the right knee for Mom. The stitches would nicely accessorize his work.

Mom detailed her personal itinerary for the good Doctor, and he was in quick agreement that she should take advantage of her plan to cruise the Caribbean in the days before surgery. Once sliced and diced, she will be landlocked for 12 weeks.

The Cruise was to depart on January 20th returning on the 27th. Surgery was scheduled for February 16th with a projected stay between five and seven days. The children and I had a combined total of at least 12 sleeps without Mom in the house. Dust could gather. Beds could remain unmade. Dishes could pile up, and lint could gather in the dryer screen. Sadly I am trained to prevent such domestic crimes against humanity.

Mom's only concern about the timing of her Cruise was that I was going to Court without her rage to keep my fighting spirits high. I would also return home alone. I wasn't alone; I had convinced myself that Mr. Date.Ca would be in my corner.

Mr. $375.00 an Hour called to remind me that Lawzilla was going after a deferral on the 25th. He assured me that though we were going to comply we would only do so with some interim financial relief.

Deferral granted. I had nothing left to lose.

Perfect Prey

Luck of the Irish

On Wednesday, January 17th the Irish Lad, a new member on www.date.ca, appeared. He e-mailed me expressing his interest to learn more about me. His profile communicated a graduate degree, business success, divorced, children who live faraway, and that he was 49. He appeared to be a large man and had a welcoming smile. I failed to notice his eyes. Still, I felt the need to follow up.

My rational for communicating with this person was simple: I was interested in dating, and Mr. Date.Ca clearly had another life; one that relegated me to week night only dates now and then. I could not tolerate dating deferrals as well. I needed to believe that if I were to continue to search, I might find happily ever after. In the meantime, dinner with Mr. Date.Ca was confirmed for Saturday night, January 20th.

Mr. Law and Order had become a distant memory, and I wanted to reignite my status as a concurrent dater. This was a defining moment. I was no further ahead in love, business, personal finances, or marital status. I responded to the Irish Lad. We instant messaged for half an hour and the banter was of the highest quality. Words coupled with clever turns of phrase have always been foreplay for me.

I was at the end of my rope and wanted the nightmare created by my ex-Husband to be over. I wanted to create my own replacement family and give my children a chance at so-called normalcy. I didn't care about falling madly in love. I just wanted to experience a little tenderness and encouragement. The road to hell is paved with good intentions and I mistook that road as being already travelled.

The Irish Lad lived within 10 kilometres of my home. I welcomed the chance to date someone that did not require me to fill up my gas tank and pack a lunch. He also worked in North Toronto, on the subway line for Universal Energy Corporation. By comparison I had learned his home address, employer location and was offered both his cell and land line telephone numbers within hours of our first communication. This seemed normal.

He suggested that I call him after 7:00 P.M. on Friday. I replied: "You are assuming I am without plans?" His response: "Am I not the only one?" That was a loaded question brimming with arrogance and self-confidence. I was in trouble. I was ripe and ready to be someone's only one. I told myself it made sense to divide my attractions as it would reduce my level of intensity and in some cases urgency. It also made sense to hedge my bets in favour of not being left in a holding pattern.

Top of the Morning to You!

Friday, January 19, 2007, 5:56 A.M. I had not anticipated a communication from the Irish Lad. I had not even wished for one. Still it came and it was brief and cheerful. He wanted me to have a great day filled with hope and joy.

My day included a visit to the lawyer's office. The coincidence was that the Irish Lad worked in the same building, but on the 16th floor. I couldn't help but wonder what fate had in store?

Perfect Prey

Seated in Mom's plain view, I telephoned the Irish Lad. It was like wearing water-wings in the bathtub. As safe as I thought I was, I forgot a simple rule: USE YOUR CELLPHONE. Instead, I dialled from my Mom's listed landline allowing my suitor to perform a reverse search and locate me.

The Irish Lad's Northern Irish accent was soothing. I remained silent throughout just to listen.

Our conversation quickly turned coincidental. His family background was, he said, Irish Jewish and Catholic as is my Mother's family. Remember, familiarity breeds contempt.

Talk of his service in the military as a Royal Marine during the Falkland Island War gave me a false sense of security.

When he began to describe his daughter, I became putty in his hands. Even her name, Siobhan, was lyrical. She was a medical student in Dublin about to write her boards and head to Toronto's Hospital for Sick Children to begin a paediatric oncology residency in July.

He spoke of the challenges they faced as father and daughter. Her Mother had abandoned the family to pursue a legal career in California. Here again, a coincidental reference to my own spouse's life choices.

He closed by saying how much he continues to marvel at his daughter's accomplishments. I responded with similar sentiments about my pride for my own daughters.

Perfect Prey

I agreed to coffee Sunday afternoon at Starbucks on Bayview Avenue, in the heart of Leaside at 2 P.M.

I had little time to think about the Irish Lad on Saturday as I had a dinner date with Mr. Date.Ca. He arrived with outstanding flowers and wine. I was genuinely touched and not my usual frantic self. I had the power of concurrent dating. It allowed me to defer my need to know his true marital status and regard him simply as a date.

Mr. Date.Ca e-mailed me on Sunday morning to thank me for my hospitality. I had worked hard on creating a memorable evening for us and felt a telephone call would have been more appropriate.

With the noon hour fast approaching I remembered that I had made a coffee date with the Irish Lad. I had regrets and feelings of great anticipation all rolled into one. I would have preferred to have had coffee with Mr. Date.Ca. Instead, I was about to meet again with the Irish Lad.

My life would never be the same.

Part 2

Lying is always a form of social control. Whether self-deception, outwardly, without awareness, or with the intent to harm, lies change everything.

The Con of Liz Cole by John Melvin Hill: The first 75 days:

Sunday, January 21, 2007

Seated by the front window in Starbucks with his back against the window was the Irish Lad. Once again, I am between a rock and a hard place. First meetings are really first rounds in a boxing ring. My footwork sucks; I forgot my mouth guard – and I sure as hell ain't a contender.

He rose to greet me and embraced me with a bear hug despite my extended hand. I must give off a "touch me" vibe. Well at least to strangers. He eased me out of my coat and pulled out my chair. In Starbuckese I would have to describe him as "Venti" rendering me "Grande" for the first time in a long-time. He had to weigh at least 270 pounds and stood about 5'10" tall. For the first time in a long while, my ass looked small.

Seconds later, he placed a steaming non fat caramel macchiato under my nose. Before I could even take a sip, he barraged me with compliments, the most memorable of which was that my dating profile picture did not do me justice. He has no idea how wrong he is.

My best photos mostly feature Santa Claus. He went on to say that every eye in Starbucks was on me. I could barely focus on what to say or do. Flattery is like oxygen for a tired heart.

Stunned, I allowed him to do most of the talking. The details of his personal life were rolled out before me, each one being more exciting than the last. He began with his roots in Southern Ireland, from Cobh, a small inlet off Cork. When I mentioned his accent seemed from the North, he responded that he had learned to alter his intonation as a survival mechanism. It was necessary for his work as a peace negotiator/consultant stationed in Belfast over the past four years. In fact, his decision to come to Canada was two-fold: resume a normal life in business to recover from work-related burnout and create a home for the pending arrival of his daughter.

In a span of 30 minutes he spoke of his time at Microsoft, adventures serving in the British Marines during the Falkland Islands, his love of large dogs, the number of times he skydived and that he still played rugby. Shifting gears, he glossed over his passion for sailing and cooking, the latter of which had him in and out of the restaurant business. I am too tired to care about every last detail – and I figure that anybody else's life story has got to be more interesting than my own. Besides, it's just coffee at Starbucks.

Toward the latter portion of our hour together he mentioned that he was on a tight schedule as he has lined up real estate appointments with the hope of buying a house.

Perfect Prey

When I invited him to ask questions about my life, he calmly tabled that discussion to our next date. *Shit, a next date. I must be giving off some kind of scent.* Then he grinned while saying that his comfort in my presence was a sign of hope for the future of his romantic life. Though he had dated over the years, he began to wonder if he would ever find genuine companionship. *Get a dog.*

I began to reach for my coat when he leaned across the table and kissed me. Apparently I blushed and he found that to be refreshing. I did not solicit this kiss nor did I want it. It just happened. He knew that he had shocked me so he arose and assisted me with my coat. We approached the door, and he offered to walk me to my car. Then he let slip that he in fact came from considerable family wealth largely achieved through his Father's international car dealership holdings. *Too much information.*

In response I said that walking me to the car would not be necessary. I had errands to run and planned on taking a long walk home. We did walk together toward his car, a new black Ford Escape. On approach, he apologized for having a common domestic vehicle but felt it prudent given the harsh winters experienced by Ontarians. I simply smiled.

It must have been after 9 P.M. when he called to talk about the houses he saw down in the Beach community. One in particular was home to a very loving and large dog, one that reminded him of his recently deceased Newfoundlander, Fred. I was intrigued by his interest to reside in the Beach community considering his work was considerably north, and not as the crow flies.

He asked me if I would be interested in helping him navigate the communities of Toronto, keeping in mind the arrival of his young professional daughter, who would be working around the clock, saving children's lives. This can't be happening. Why hasn't someone more suitable to his life experience and background snatched him up? I mean hoisted him up given his weight. Now that smacks of being kind of judgmental for a woman living in her Mommy's house.

I noted the time and it was late. I thought I'd take a chance and ask him a question about his business contacts as I was in the market for a publisher. Rather than ask me about the nature of my writing project. he immediately began to reference countless friends and cousins – ironically all named Seamus – from Ireland, New York and England. Following a brief pause, he determined one of two possible courses of action. The first would be to connect me with the Irish Seamus and second would be to introduce me to his friend, the Editor-in-Chief at Canadian Living.

I asked him what his connection was to the good people at Canadian Living particularly since he was in the energy business. He replied that they were located on the first floor of his office building and that a friendship was formed, first over lobby chit chat, and finally through his expertise as a chef. Apparently they welcomed him into their test kitchens. What I didn't mention was that my Mother was a retired Canadian Living employee and was indeed a friendly acquaintance of the Editor-in-Chief. Nor did I mention that my lawyer was on the 7th floor.

The Irish Lad made his goodbye referencing that he was truly smitten with me. Google John Hill. Now that's a genius idea. Why not Google John Smith.

Monday, January 22, 2007

My day began with a phone call at 7:15 A.M. Someone's dead. That's how it works when the phone rings early in the day or late at night.

The Irish Lad was on a mission. He wanted to see me this evening. I had to decline. Tess has dance, Rachel has homework and I am wiped out. Besides, I was in training for the Family Court Deferral Olympics.

The Irish Lad called again at 10:45 A.M. He just wanted me to know that he had been peddling my wellness wares throughout his corporate offices and to expect follow up. I thanked him and suggested we'd talk later in the day.

I couldn't even remember talking about my wellness business as he did all the talking.

Today wore on, like most days only this day came with a change of heart. I e-mailed the Irish Lad suggesting that we meet for coffee with the understanding that I only had one hour while Tess was at dance class. He was immediately receptive and we agreed on a time/location rendezvous. As we approached each other on the street, I couldn't help but notice that his arms began to open as if to be welcoming me into his heart. *BEAR HUG incoming. Prepare for a punctured lung.*

Perfect Prey

We decided to pass on coffee in favour of wine and appetizers at a nearby bistro. We saddled up to the bar and made small talk with the bartender. She asked us how long we had been a couple because we seemed so in sync. For me, it's not possible to be in sync with anyone – and I have the track record to prove it.

Between sips and nibbles, we kissed. *I know, too soon. I'm not even a cheap drunk.* I only had one glass of wine. It just seemed right. The Irish Lad reached for my left hand and asked me for my ring size. I suggested we have a meal together before booking the church. The hour went by and he walked me to my van outside the dance studio. He commented on how a busy single mother should drive a better vehicle for reasons of safety and comfort. *I know. That's why I have a divorce lawyer.* We managed to steal one more kiss before he slipped away into the night leaving my daughter none the wiser.

Wednesday, January 24

A hard day indeed. Totally wiped out today. Not such a big deal for a clinically depressed premenopausal woman.

The Irish Lad was too good to be true based on my dating history including marriage. Surely he could do better. This is not self pity. Happily ever after is not on my radar, in the cards, my horoscope, or tattooed on my ass.

Mr. Date.Ca continued to e-mail me, but clearly forgot about my Court date and all its implications. How is it possible that this man could forget such an important detail? I guess I should ask: Important to whom?

Susan spent a good portion of the day in my company rather that working for our company. She even treated me to lunch. I was in a fog. I needed a round at Curves, but couldn't muster the energy to workout much less take the dog for a walk. I needed a hug. I needed Mr. Date.Ca to drop everything and give me a hug.

Mr. Date.Ca's lack of effort is wearing on me. I have stayed off-line to see if he cares enough to pick up a phone. I don't have the time and energy to play this kind of game. Maybe I should forfeit.

In the hours before Court, I e-mailed Mr. Date.Ca to remind him that I was in fact on my way to Court. How pathetic am I? He wished me luck. He had no idea that I had the Luck of the Irish.

I called the Irish Lad and suggested dinner out on Thursday night. He accepted.

I cried a lot today. I know Tess and Rachel saw me. I know they see the fear in my eyes. I know they do not understand why their Father won't do the right thing and provide consistent support for his children. They are watching my every move and I need to wow them. They need Mommy to walk into the courtroom and come out a champion. They have no idea their basic rights will be deferred.

I am pushing too hard. Making lists helps calm me down. It borders on obsessive-compulsive, but helps me to slow my thoughts and avoid making poor decisions. I need to organize tomorrow, at least in my mind:

1. Make lunches for the girls.
2. Serve breakfast to the girls.
3. Hit the shower.
4. Book an appointment for new brakes.
5. Go to Court.
6. Succeed in Court.
7. Return home, collapse and rise again.
8. Have dinner with the Irish Lad.

Perfect Prey

Thursday, January 25, 2007

The Irish Lad called me at 5:30 A.M. to wish me great luck in Court. I swear to God he uttered the words, "I love you." How is this even possible? How is it possible that my Husband could hate me so much; Mr. Date.Ca is so indifferent and now this oversized leprechaun tells me that he loves me.

We got off to a good start in Court. The Judge reordered the caseload placing my file in first position. This change in scheduling means less billable time by Mr. $375.00 an Hour and saved me a couple of parking bucks.

My Husband has entangled all of us in a legal nightmare. I wish you could have seen Lawzilla. She is the angriest-looking-and-acting human being I have ever faced. She's a legal dinosaur prone to tantrums. Her use of theatrics may entertain the peanut gallery, but clearly angered the Judge.

Lawzilla sought a lengthy continuance, allowing my Husband to continue to neglect us. Our position was to grant this motion without prejudice with terms. They were granted two months. Mr. $375.00 an Hour made it clear that we were not leaving without some financial reparation for the children. We got it. Better than nothing.

I saw Lawzilla sucking the life out of a cigarette while seated outside the courthouse on a cement stair. It was so bitterly cold out that I was sure she'd end up with a pile of hemorrhoids maybe even a bladder infection. I asked God to grant me the power to give this woman a burning sensation she'd never forget. I think I am still in the game. Lawzilla had to phone her client and tell him to cough up $5,000 and let him know that she was unable to cancel his membership as a Father and Husband.

The Judge did affirm Lawzilla's right to conduct an interrogation on February 6th. Despite my complete personal and financial disclosure, stated expenses, and projected expenses not to mention my Husband's decision to end the marriage, she was determined to get to the bottom of my evil ways. *Note to self: Get evil ways.*

Tonight's dinner date plans with the Irish Lad never happened. He left me an apologetic message about having some sort of work conflict. No biggie. I do rejection well.

I must have grown a spine today because I called him back and said that it was a big deal to cancel.

Mr. Date.Ca slithered through cyberspace to say hello. *Big mistake: Pick up the phone you asshole.*

Friday, January 26, 2007

Today came and went without word from the Irish Lad and that is not kosher. I began to take refuge in a litre of candy cane ice cream. Thank God for girlfriends. I had a great lunch date with my girlfriend who works for the Ontario Provincial Police, the same friend who set me up with Mr. Law and Order. We agreed not to speak his name.

Mr. Date.Ca's office was across the street from the restaurant and I risked a truce by calling with the suggestion that I pay him a visit.

He apologized for not recognizing the seriousness of my situation and responding properly. Damage had been done this time and I could not tolerate more disappointment and frustration. Still, I remained in his presence for an hour or so followed by a round of pinball in the company games room. As good a time as it was, I knew that when I left that building it was over. *There I said it. We were over. I should have told him.*

Saturday, January 27, 2007

While on line earlier today, I noticed the Irish Lad was live so I asked him why he hadn't followed through with his plans to see me. He spoke of loyalty and trust. He suggested that I downplayed my anxiety and pain to appear strong and in control. He said this wasn't being honest and was a red flag for him because trust was central for a successful relationship.

I quickly let him know that he had no right to direct any assumptions or judgments my way as he hardly even knew me. He backed down immediately and was very apologetic, citing that his most recent past relationship has failed because of the other party's dishonesty. *Sweet Mother of God we have baggage!*

He suggested that I join him for a glass of wine at his home around 8 P.M. The address was familiar and reasonably close by. This invitation came with a warning that his temporary basement apartment was a stopgap on the way to a permanent home with his daughter. This living arrangement was a benefit for him as it was based on a month-to-month agreement. It also served as a favour to a friend in need.

The Lad overwhelmed me at his side door with a bone crushing hug. The sudden lack of oxygen didn't help make his apartment look better. In fact, the absence of air in my lungs made it possible for me to disguise my overwhelming disappointment with his digs. Good deeds aside, this place was nothing short of student housing. He was right about the appearance of the apartment in that it was clean and sparsely furnished. It was a temporary respite for people interested in passing through. The location was the charm. *Fuck location, my head keeps hitting his ceiling.*

The Lad talked, and I listened to his story connecting his rugby chum to his living arrangements. Apparently, the chum had to return to Vancouver making it impossible to keep a close eye on his aging Father, afflicted with Alzheimer's. The Father did live with his life partner, an able and delightful woman, but the changes in his Father's health made the day to day reality increasingly challenging for her. The plan was to hire a live in caregiver. The perfect plan would to have both a caregiver for his Father as well as an able bodied male in the house as an additional security measure.

The Irish Lad insisted the measure of his life was about being of service to others. *Women of the world unite: I have just received a breaking news story that suggests our collective lives of service have moved us to the front of the line either for welfare or heaven.* At best, he was only going to live in this basement apartment until the end of March. He had been living there since the beginning of November. By then, a reliable caregiver would be in place and the Rugby friend would have time to make other arrangements for his Father, if necessary. Helping a friend made the offer irresistible to him.

I was a little weirded out by the absence of any personal doo-dads or photographs. Naturally, I felt the need to tell him that I found his existence to appear cold and impersonal. And I'll be damned if he reminded me that our lives were similarly tied up in storage. *Correction Irish Lad, my life is tied up in Court!*

The Irish Lad opened a bottle of Argentinean wine noting that while it was not pricey, it was satisfying. It also gave way to the subject of Argentina, and stories about his life as a Major serving in the Falkland Islands.

I found myself being interviewed about the nature of my work and the clients served along with questions pertaining to the kind of income wellness consultants would typically achieve. The latter part was none of his business and I told him so. *Duh? I live with my Mother and drive an eight year old mini van.* He had surmised that a minimum income of $100,000 would be necessary to live safely in Toronto. *Wanna bet?* I smiled and made no comment.

I ended our evening seconds shy of 11:00 P.M. He walked me to my car and watched me pull away. Minutes into the ride, he called me on my cell phone thanking me for the visit and to travel safely.

Sunday, January 28, 2007

Spent the afternoon with the Irish Lad in his apartment and was served great appetizers and wine. With my mouth full, most of the time, I let him ramble on about his role as a Sales Director for Universal Energy Corporation. I was curious how he came to find this job given his most recent work as a peace negotiator in Belfast.

Apparently his friends and contacts in the Jewish community welcomed him into their fold. *Note to Christians: get a community to fall back on.* He had reconnected with this side of his roots by joining the Jewish Community Centre on arrival to Toronto. The conversation boiled down to the adage: "It's not what you know, but who you know."

I asked him about his connection to our mutual online dating site. Smiling he said that his membership was a gift from the partners' wives. Initially, they had enrolled him on www.jdate.com, the site for Jewish singles. He had managed to meet a small number of women, but found their materialistic expectations to be off-putting. His wealth was not his calling card. He soon realized that this arm of the dating site allowed for lateral movement into the main site, www.date.ca.

He asked me about my own dating history remarking that he found it difficult to believe that I was not busy with a number of suitors. *I am busy with a number of suitors; it's just that they need to ask their ex wives permission to date me on weekend nights.*

I reminded him that I was 44, lived with my Mom, and had two teenaged daughters, a one-eyed dog and enough divorce related drama to last a lifetime. I further revealed that I wanted love and to establish a normal family life but recognized that there is a time and place for everything. *Lotto 649 would pretty much nail down the lesser details.*

As relaxed as I was in the Lad's sub dwelling, I knew that Mom was returning to Toronto today. The "to-do" list was etched on my forehead: Remove all traces of life that suggest we live with her. Make ice cubes.

The flight was on time, but the baggage carousel was on the fritz. *Holy shit, that describes my entire battle with infertility.*

I managed to confine my update to my experience in Court and the increasing presence of the Irish Lad. Exhausted and hesitant, Mom lent me her ear. Somehow that seemed fair as I had lent her my mini-van for airport pick up service.

Thursday, February 1, 2007

Wiped out again. Work, chores, parenting, legal nonsense and now there was this 270 pound leprechaun to deal with. He had a hectic work-week and could not visit with me until tonight.

The Hurricane, as Mom called him, blew into all of our lives and changed our world from that moment forward. Mom had met her match. He talked her good ear off. Seated in Mom's living room, it was apparent that he was holding court. Stories about far away places, social connections and personal aspirations for his life in Toronto had Tess and Rachel on the edge of their seat. He concluded his broadcast with a few key words: "I love your Mother."

It was ridiculous and though I knew it, I wanted to believe that someone could love me, that anyone could love me. Then he blew out the door – a refreshing change from being completely blown off.

Friday, February 2, 2007

Today was all about drama. The Lad burst through the front door and was on a mission. He was anticipating a full agenda for the balance of the weekend related to finding a house. I was to be riding shotgun as both navigator and neighbourhood advisor. Despite our invitation for him to sit for a while and have something to eat, he was too excited, manic really, and wanted to return to his home to download the listings being forwarded by his agent. On this occasion, we would only visit listings during their weekend open house times. Follow up appointments would be determined based on "our" interest.

As crazy as this all seemed to me, it was a marvellous distraction from what lay ahead. I knew that in four short days, I would be in lock down, in a court reporting office with Lawzilla. I also knew that in 14 shorts days, my Mother would be having knee replacement surgery and my commitment to her recovery would limit my free time for such antics.

The Irish Lad had landed. Mom may have had her misgivings about the genuineness of his affections for me but seemed to believe that his self-proclaimed wealth was on the up and up. Even she suggested that he confine his search to established neighbourhoods such as Forest Hill, Leaside, Rosedale and the Hoggs Hollow. When the Lad referenced the Kingsway, Mom's reaction, though favourable was cautionary as it was too far from Leaside. It was at that point that she connected us as a couple. It was a backhanded blessing of sorts.

The Irish Lad reminded us that we had to be careful to identify locations that would accommodate his daughter's demanding medical career schedule. We all nodded. Praise be to the Irish Lad. Our liberator had come.

Saturday February 3, 2007

The Hurricane blew back in with bouquets of flowers for each of us. He had taken the time to select individual bouquets based on their respective attributes and further link them with each of us. Mom received an arrangement in varying shades of purple denoting royalty. Tess received petal pink roses for their delicacy. Rachel was a burst of colours as was she. My own bouquet, a dozen red roses implying love. Then he handed me a whack of real estate listings.

Mom asked to speak to me in private. She needed to confirm that he alone was buying a house.

The Irish Lad had a better than average sense of Toronto's major streets and communities. My role was to organize the open house listings in a way that made good use of our time and geography. We were on our way and I could not overlook the fact that the listings ranged in price from $800,000 to $1.2 million. My appreciation for the listings in their respective neighbourhoods was deemed useful. The problem was that the price range based on location resulted in modestly sized homes. By that I mean three bedrooms, two bathrooms, dated basements, kitchens etc. He was disappointed. It became clear that he would either have to increase his budget or pursue a broader range of communities.

The house had to be large enough for him to live, entertain and provide Siobhan, his daughter with living and working quarters complete with private bath.

We returned to the car and resumed our search. I was amused. This was not my life or my money. I was also sad because I once had my own dream house and knew that was then and this was now. Without warning. the Irish Lad pulled the car over to the curb and cut the engine. Startled, I asked him if we had missed something and needed to turn around. He replied: "Yes, I missed something. Before we go any further looking for the right house, I want to know if you see yourself living in any one of them. I want to know if you will marry me?"

"Are you nuts?" I replied.

Perfect Prey

Mom asked to speak to me in private. She needed to confirm that he alone was buying a house.

The Irish Lad had a better than average sense of Toronto's major streets and communities. My role was to organize the open house listings in a way that made good use of our time and geography. We were on our way and I could not overlook the fact that the listings ranged in price from $800,000 to $1.2 million. My appreciation for the listings in their respective neighbourhoods was deemed useful. The problem was that the price range based on location resulted in modestly sized homes. By that I mean three bedrooms, two bathrooms, dated basements, kitchens etc. He was disappointed. It became clear that he would either have to increase his budget or pursue a broader range of communities.

The house had to be large enough for him to live, entertain and provide Siobhan, his daughter with living and working quarters complete with private bath.

We returned to the car and resumed our search. I was amused. This was not my life or my money. I was also sad because I once had my own dream house and knew that was then and this was now. Without warning. the Irish Lad pulled the car over to the curb and cut the engine. Startled, I asked him if we had missed something and needed to turn around. He replied: "Yes, I missed something. Before we go any further looking for the right house, I want to know if you see yourself living in any one of them. I want to know if you will marry me?"

"Are you nuts?" I replied.

shorts days, my Mother would be having knee replacement surgery and my commitment to her recovery would limit my free time for such antics.

The Irish Lad had landed. Mom may have had her misgivings about the genuineness of his affections for me but seemed to believe that his self-proclaimed wealth was on the up and up. Even she suggested that he confine his search to established neighbourhoods such as Forest Hill, Leaside, Rosedale and the Hoggs Hollow. When the Lad referenced the Kingsway, Mom's reaction, though favourable was cautionary as it was too far from Leaside. It was at that point that she connected us as a couple. It was a backhanded blessing of sorts.

The Irish Lad reminded us that we had to be careful to identify locations that would accommodate his daughter's demanding medical career schedule. We all nodded. Praise be to the Irish Lad. Our liberator had come.

Saturday February 3, 2007

The Hurricane blew back in with bouquets of flowers for each of us. He had taken the time to select individual bouquets based on their respective attributes and further link them with each of us. Mom received an arrangement in varying shades of purple denoting royalty. Tess received petal pink roses for their delicacy. Rachel was a burst of colours as was she. My own bouquet, a dozen red roses implying love. Then he handed me a whack of real estate listings.

He remained steadfast, but said he would settle for a promise from me to at least commit to the possibility of becoming his bride.

This was insanity. A flood of thoughts raced through my mind. I asked myself: *Who is this man? Why me? Why not me?*

The search for houses came to an abrupt end. I couldn't think about anything. I was also hungry and thirsty. Before I knew it we were seated in a local pub, The Abbott. The Irish Lad was thrilled by the choice of restaurants and the higher end range of classic pub traditions. The server approached and asked us for our drink order. I ordered a glass of wine, while he ordered Irish ale of some sort. Then, he asked the server to assist him with the task of buying a round for the staff as he was celebrating his engagement to me.

The Irish Lad knew I was not divorced. He did not accept my decision to table this offer at a much later time. He started the party instead.

My brain went into an uncontrollable spasm. I could not focus and I could not reason. I could only see the possibility of living happily ever after. I had never experienced love at first sight and I knew that I was not experiencing love now. I was tripping. I was rationalizing my personal despair as grounds, indeed substitution, for love. It didn't matter that I did not feel love. It mattered that someone could love me. That would be enough.

The Hurricane dropped me off at Mom's later in the afternoon suggesting that I take a few hours to catch my breath. I also needed to tell her everything. She warned me to be careful. That was an understatement.

The plan for tonight was to return to his home, make dinner and if possible, for me to stay over. You have no idea how weird it is to tell your Mom that your plans may include a test drive of the merchandise.

I made my way to his home and clutched the first of several glasses of wine. The Irish Lad initiated the evening's conversation, as usual. Tonight he talked about his stock options as an employee of Universal Energy Products. He had alleged to have bought 33,400 shares of Universal product at $9.00 per share. In addition to this timely acquisition he also spoke very highly about his investment person, at Scotia McLeod. Irish Lad John spoke of him as though they were long-time associates. He rewarded his professionalism with the responsibility of managing his significant portfolio.

I had to use every muscle in my face to conceal my surprise. Not because he could buy that many stocks, but because I knew that he was my Mom's investment person as well.

Sunday, February 4, 2007

I can't even remember how many open houses we torpedoed through. I must have been nuts to tag along for the entire day knowing that I'd promised to cook dinner for family, the Lad and Mom's friend, Joanie-Joan. *Yes, Joanie-Joan.*

I do remember flying through Mom's door and right into the kitchen. Precious seconds were saved by virtue of the fact that the wine had already been opened. His

Perfect Prey

voice in the background was only the sound. The women sat at attention while he narrated the story of his ever fascinating life to date. A new audience meant revitalization for the Hurricane. I could hear Auntie Joanie-Joan sigh and gasp as he detailed the nature of his medical discharge from the British Marines. Stories about his days as an expert chef and restaurant owner in Vancouver did create a certain feeling of pressure while I prepared the meal in Mom's kitchen. I was too busy to worry and stay standing at the same time.

Then the family history was revealed starting with his father, Ken Hill an extraordinary business man who owned in varying percentages over 30 car dealerships throughout the United Kingdom, Montreal and Ottawa. His paternal Grandfather was an investment banker credited with starting the first investment bank in Cork, Ireland. His self-professed wealth had captured the attention of the room, and I would be a liar if I said that money didn't matter. I had lost everything and my soon-to-be ex-Husband was spending very little of his money on his children.

The Irish Lad changed gears and began to express his intention to replace my minivan. He had already spoken with his Father expressing his affection for me and his plans for our future. In response his Father wanted to gift me a new vehicle. The Lad suggested Mom give up her 1992 raspberry red Plymouth Sundance and assume his new Ford Escape as he was about to take possession of an Audi A6. *Everybody wins.*

He never stopped long enough to invite questions.
Dinner was served. I prepared racks of ribs, roasted red potatoes seasoned with rosemary and orange maple

carrots. I cook like this every night and clean the house while wearing pearls.

Tuesday, February 6, 2007

I had little hope for this day but was pleasantly surprised by the quality of the muffins and coffee that were served in the court reporting offices.

Mr. $375.00 an Hour was at my side and guided my recordable remarks in such a way as to not let me incriminate myself. He was paid to prevent me from calling Lawzilla a venomous bitch. He also prevented me from ripping her throat out. What he can't seem to do is prevent me from crying uncontrollably as the injustice continues to impact my children's lives.

The Irish Lad had briefly coached me the night before. It seems that his years as a negotiator taught him a thing or two about how to sustain a non-responsive facial expression. He reminded me about keeping my eyes fixed on Lawzilla at all times, and, if I was feeling too much pressure, I could always request a bathroom break. When all else failed, offer up a Cheshire cat grin. The transcripts would not reveal facial expressions, just words. I know this is a powerful suggestion as 55 per cent of all significant human communication is conveyed through our body language, followed by our tone of voice.

This meeting was to last all day and cost me a small fortune. It ended after two hours. My facts were in order and unchanging. Their plan had failed.

Wednesday, February 7, 2007

I spent today in Collingwood preparing for the arrival of a family that had offered to rent the property for a long weekend. I had invited the Irish Lad to tag along. He was too committed to advancing work assignments but promised he'd call often. He told me how much he loved me. Maybe it's just me, but when I hear a man tell me that he loves me, my mind wanders to follow-up comments such as: "The cheque is in the mail," or "It will clear up your skin." I haven't heard the word love in such a long time, though I have spoken it without ever hearing a response.

The Lad called to ensure my safe arrival. We talked about work and how he planned to grab some take-away food on his way home from work. The expert chef grabbed a lot of take-away food a lot of the time.

Thursday, February 8, 2007

The Irish Lad was on the phone, speaking in the voice of a very ill man. He said the take-away chicken had levelled him. He was mustering up the strength to make his way to a local walk-in clinic to receive a shot of gravol. From there he planned to go to work. The diagnosis was food poisoning and a massive dose of antibiotics was prescribed to ward off the danger associated with the infecting bacteria. I thought about heading home to be at his side then realized he still planned to make it to work.

I needed the rest from all that awaited me in Toronto. I would return Friday as planned.

Perfect Prey

Friday, February 9. 2007

Complaining of feeling awful, and of being plagued with nausea, vomiting, and diarrhoea, the Irish Lad asked that I leave him to suffer in silence, and I did.

Early that evening, Rachel needed a ride to a friend's house located in the Bathurst Street and Lawrence Avenue area. It was about 7:30 P.M. I was on route home having dropped her off when out of no where, a black Ford Escape pulled in front of me, and then returned to the lane beside me. We were at a red light. I looked out my passenger side window only to see the Irish Lad stopped beside me.

I lowered the window and asked him why he wasn't at home? He replied: "I had to work late and now I am coming to see you." I said: "Don't bother." He did, in fact, look well.

I am so tired of chauffeuring, hosting, dating, cooking, cleaning, struggling and God help me, living. Maybe that seems selfish; maybe I should be counting my blessings and recall that my life of service, as the Lad calls it, is its own reward. From where I sit, if my efforts don't start racking up reward miles then I'm cutting up the card. Or at the very least I will ask a Family Court Judge where I should go to redeem my points.

Friday, February 9. 2007

Complaining of feeling awful, and of being plagued with nausea, vomiting, and diarrhoea, the Irish Lad asked that I leave him to suffer in silence, and I did.

Early that evening, Rachel needed a ride to a friend's house located in the Bathurst Street and Lawrence Avenue area. It was about 7:30 P.M. I was on route home having dropped her off when out of no where, a black Ford Escape pulled in front of me, and then returned to the lane beside me. We were at a red light. I looked out my passenger side window only to see the Irish Lad stopped beside me.

I lowered the window and asked him why he wasn't at home? He replied: "I had to work late and now I am coming to see you." I said: "Don't bother." He did, in fact, look well.

I am so tired of chauffeuring, hosting, dating, cooking, cleaning, struggling and God help me, living. Maybe that seems selfish; maybe I should be counting my blessings and recall that my life of service, as the Lad calls it, is its own reward. From where I sit, if my efforts don't start racking up reward miles then I'm cutting up the card. Or at the very least I will ask a Family Court Judge where I should go to redeem my points.

Wednesday, February 7, 2007

I spent today in Collingwood preparing for the arrival of a family that had offered to rent the property for a long weekend. I had invited the Irish Lad to tag along. He was too committed to advancing work assignments but promised he'd call often. He told me how much he loved me. Maybe it's just me, but when I hear a man tell me that he loves me, my mind wanders to follow-up comments such as: "The cheque is in the mail," or "It will clear up your skin." I haven't heard the word love in such a long time, though I have spoken it without ever hearing a response.

The Lad called to ensure my safe arrival. We talked about work and how he planned to grab some take-away food on his way home from work. The expert chef grabbed a lot of take-away food a lot of the time.

Thursday, February 8, 2007

The Irish Lad was on the phone, speaking in the voice of a very ill man. He said the take-away chicken had levelled him. He was mustering up the strength to make his way to a local walk-in clinic to receive a shot of gravol. From there he planned to go to work. The diagnosis was food poisoning and a massive dose of antibiotics was prescribed to ward off the danger associated with the infecting bacteria. I thought about heading home to be at his side then realized he still planned to make it to work.

I needed the rest from all that awaited me in Toronto. I would return Friday as planned.

Perfect Prey

Monday, February 12, 2007

Bright-eyed and bushy tailed, the Hurricane, AKA Irish Lad John Hill, breezed through Mom's front door minutes before I had to drive Tess to dance class. Both Mom and I were encouraged by his return to the land of the living. Again, he was on a mission. Having just wrapped up on-line travel plans, we were all booked for travel to Dublin, London and Paris leaving August 16th. Astounded by the gesture, we allowed the Irish Lad centre stage and he rose quickly to the spotlight.

Tess and Rachel were literally shrieking with delight. Our current living arrangements, coupled with my debt, had rendered us all landlocked. It's amazing how short my daughters' memories are having just returned from their Florida vacations? The Irish Lad had the key. He spoke of the shops in Paris and the requirement for every young woman to own at least one original garment in her lifetime. Then he spoke of the pubs in Ireland and how teens were welcome to have a diluted pint with their elders. Reference to his country and city homes intrigued all of us. The question remained: Why?

Why indeed. The plan was to celebrate our life together as a family and to make the necessary introductions befitting this new life. In Paris we would meet his estranged Mother. His parents had divorced when he was 10 for the simple reason that she had revealed her homosexuality and wanted to re-establish herself along with her lover in Paris. In this new life she would go on to forge a brilliant alternative newspaper for the gay community.

The Irish Lad's father had remarried and produced two daughters. It turns out that his stepmother was the same age as the Lad. There was no love lost between them. To conclude his broadcast he suggested that my Mom escort the girls back to Toronto after two weeks in Europe allowing the new Mr. and Mrs. Irish Lad to remain for an additional honeymoon week. We sat still and nodded like bobble heads.

Valentine's Day

Mom spent most of the day preparing to be admitted to the Holland Orthopedic and Arthritic Centre for right knee replacement surgery on February 16th. In truth we had everything in order down to the drawstring sweat pants and National Enquirers.

The Irish Lad had agreed to join us for dinner. Valentine's Dinner, my least favourite day of the year. I can't help but flash back to 2005 when my Husband bought the children and I the same treat. Don't get me wrong, Smarties in a heart shaped box are uniquely Canadian and I love sucking off the candy coating or using the red ones to create pretend lipstick – but doesn't that seem a little weird to you?

Standing in Mom's hallway sporting a dozen red roses and a number of greeting cards was the Irish Lad, the world's largest Cupid. Mom snatched up the roses and began to arrange them in a vase while I made every attempt to rally the troops for dinner. The Irish Lad handed out his selection of cards. In common, we all received the message of his unbreakable love. Two divorced woman and two teenaged female children abandoned by their Father, what possible behaviour could result from that? The Irish Lad created a feeding frenzy. It was as if the Lad threw fish parts into a shark

Perfect Prey

pool. Within seconds of our opening the cards, he added the cards came with the promise of a *spa* day. He would defer to my knowledge of such things and leave it with me to book our day.

In the past two weeks we have been offered cars, travel, and a new house and yet the gesture of a spa day sent me over the edge. I don't think my reaction had anything to do with the Irish Lad's generosity. It was the stark contrast of his generosity to the neglect of my Husband that created such pain.

I know I appeared unappreciative. I didn't care. I didn't want to be rescued. I wanted to remain angry at my Husband. I guess I couldn't see that it was possible to fight for the rights of my children and have a pedicure. Living well is the best revenge, says the Lad.

Friday, February 16, 2007

Few days begin well with the awareness that surgery is on the "to-do" list. Mom was mentally and physically prepared to make her way to the hospital with me at her side. Her surgeon suggested that she would be resting comfortably in her room by 1:00 P.M. True, if the operation was being performed on the West Coast; 4:00 P.M. for those of us in Ontario.

I paced the halls like an expectant Father. Then, I rifled through the meal carts to see what was on the menu and to pilfer what was left behind. It would appear that bananas lacked popularity. Mom's return to the room came as a sweet relief. I no longer had to find ways to amuse myself. Now I had a heavily medicated person to talk to. I lingered for a few hours, helped her with her dinner and left behind a whack of gossip rags and liquorice. For the record, liquorice is nature's remedy for constipation according to my Mom. I do not believe the strawberry twists are as effective unless you bite the ends off and use the straw like candy as a means to deliver an enema. Gross!

Saturday, February 17, 2007

The Irish Lad insisted that he go with me to the hospital to visit Mom today.

He picked me up with treats in hand. Chocolates for the girls and a house key cut on a vanity key painted with shamrocks. The message that came with the key was two-fold: Escape from the madness and seek refuge in my apartment and, start getting used to living under the same roof.

We made it to Mom's hospital room for 11:00 A.M. Seconds in the door, the Irish Lad had her in full embrace and slipped her an overly affectionate greeting card that wished her a speedy recovery and signed it with much love. His gift was to cover her in-room television rental for the week.

I was visibly tired and welcomed the opportunity for the Lad to tell stories about the old country. His time as a boy in southern Ireland had forged many memories and helpful social connections for moving forward. As groggy as Mom was, the Hurricane managed to override the fog of her morphine drip by mentioning his long time friend Hilary Weston, whom he affectionately referred to as Hilsey. Their roots made it possible for them to remain available to each other, should either of them ever require a shoulder to cry on, or a laugh to share. Being a commoner, all I could think about was her connection to Loblaws and would have settled for free groceries for a month.

The Irish Lad suggested that my social calendar was about to pick up considerably and that my wardrobe, such that it was, would require Holt Renfrew's intervention. Though she was not present, I could sense Tess weeping tears of joy. Finally, the horror that is my wardrobe was to be overhauled.

Mom's head was spinning, as was mine. Our visit of several hours had reached the end. Mom was exhausted and it was time to go. Mom welcomed the peace and quiet. Her stay offered hot and good bedside meal delivery and a semi-private room without a roommate. The alternative was to return to her home and the chaos that ensued. That reality was inevitable and best stored in the back of her mind.

I was exhausted and would have given anything to just go home and sleep away the weekend.

The Irish Lad had other plans. He insisted that we make a trip to an Irish store to select a Cladagh ring. I was not interested. He was visibly ticked off. He suggested that I was acting like a spoiled brat. He was wrong. I was acting like a middle-aged single Mom clinging to her pride.

The Lad continued to drive toward the waterfront. He forgot to mention that he was facing a deadline and had to select the ideal yacht club for his 41 foot sailboat. This side trip would not take long, just a drive-by to scope out one of two options.

His sailboat was in temporary storage at the Port Credit Yacht Club. The Royal Canadian Yacht Club was his first choice because it offered so many amenities including an in-town club ideal for entertaining clients.

We ended up at the St. Lawrence Market to fetch top-drawer meat, cheeses, veggies and breads. Impressed by the market, he went on and on about how the marketplaces in Ireland were far superior. *Then go back to Ireland.*

Blocks away from Mom's home, we agreed that an infusion of Starbucks was a good idea. Settled into my comfy chair, clutching my macchiato, the Lad hurried me back to the car chirping we had one last errand to complete.

I just wanted to go home, and didn't expect what followed. The Irish Lad had made arrangements for me to test drive a Mercedes at our local dealership. He made it clear that my minivan days were numbered. His Father was quite incensed about my car, its age and wear and tear. *Maybe he should check out my ass; it's looking a little overrun too!*

The expectation was that my automotive experience, moving forward, would be up-market.

The salesperson was helpful and surprisingly empathetic. He knew that I was a stranger in a strange land. He suggested that I gather a number of brochures and return when I felt better prepared. The Irish Lad did manage to grab various car brochures to continue to make the sale over the next several hours.

His sailboat was in temporary storage at the Port Credit Yacht Club. The Royal Canadian Yacht Club was his first choice because it offered so many amenities including an in-town club ideal for entertaining clients.

We ended up at the St. Lawrence Market to fetch top-drawer meat, cheeses, veggies and breads. Impressed by the market, he went on and on about how the marketplaces in Ireland were far superior. *Then go back to Ireland.*

Blocks away from Mom's home, we agreed that an infusion of Starbucks was a good idea. Settled into my comfy chair, clutching my macchiato, the Lad hurried me back to the car chirping we had one last errand to complete.

I just wanted to go home, and didn't expect what followed. The Irish Lad had made arrangements for me to test drive a Mercedes at our local dealership. He made it clear that my minivan days were numbered. His Father was quite incensed about my car, its age and wear and tear. *Maybe he should check out my ass; it's looking a little overrun too!*

The expectation was that my automotive experience, moving forward, would be up-market.

The salesperson was helpful and surprisingly empathetic. He knew that I was a stranger in a strange land. He suggested that I gather a number of brochures and return when I felt better prepared. The Irish Lad did manage to grab various car brochures to continue to make the sale over the next several hours.

or a laugh to share. Being a commoner, all I could think about was her connection to Loblaws and would have settled for free groceries for a month.

The Irish Lad suggested that my social calendar was about to pick up considerably and that my wardrobe, such that it was, would require Holt Renfrew's intervention. Though she was not present, I could sense Tess weeping tears of joy. Finally, the horror that is my wardrobe was to be overhauled.

Mom's head was spinning, as was mine. Our visit of several hours had reached the end. Mom was exhausted and it was time to go. Mom welcomed the peace and quiet. Her stay offered hot and good bedside meal delivery and a semi-private room without a roommate. The alternative was to return to her home and the chaos that ensued. That reality was inevitable and best stored in the back of her mind.

I was exhausted and would have given anything to just go home and sleep away the weekend.

The Irish Lad had other plans. He insisted that we make a trip to an Irish store to select a Cladagh ring. I was not interested. He was visibly ticked off. He suggested that I was acting like a spoiled brat. He was wrong. I was acting like a middle-aged single Mom clinging to her pride.

The Lad continued to drive toward the waterfront. He forgot to mention that he was facing a deadline and had to select the ideal yacht club for his 41 foot sailboat. This side trip would not take long, just a drive-by to scope out one of two options.

I inhaled two glasses of wine while the Lad read aloud the features of the various cars in the promotional brochures and then we cooked dinner. The Irish Lad had to read everything aloud, to the point of becoming annoying. He loved the sound of his own voice. *It's funny how an accent can seem charming one moment and like finger nails on a chalkboard the next.*

His parting words suggested that I become open to Land Rovers.

Sunday, February 18, 2007

CRAZY DAY!

Mom was my priority along with driving carpool for Rachel's theatre program. Still I allowed the Irish Lad to book three real estate appointments followed by a quick test-drive at a Land Rover dealership.

I had caught a glimpse of myself in the rearview mirror of Land Rover and was disappointed to see that even up-market rearview mirrors don't hide exhaustion

There is truth to the expression: "You can dress me up, but can't take me out." I know that I am being offered the keys to the kingdom but the bills I have to pay are due tomorrow. The money I earn pales in comparison to my legal fees, line of credit debt associated with Rachel's education, the carrying costs of Collingwood and that little thing called food. I am supporting the monthly expenses for our insurance, storage unit, Collingwood condo fees, utilities and taxes, as well as pay for our long-term moving company storage.

Given all my living costs and many bills to pay, test driving luxury cars doesn't really make a damn bit of difference.

I am aware that the Irish Lad never leaves my side. He manages to place the right hug and the right kiss at the right time. He helps with homework and with the cooking. I just wish he'd stop talking for a minute or two. Actually, I wish he'd just buy a damn house and get on with it.

Monday, February 19, 2007

The Irish Lad had a falling-out at his job and quit. He quit a job that was the by-product of so-called social connections. There was no discussion. He just quit. He told me that Universal Energy Corporation would honour his commissions. *It was as if he was reassuring me.*

I needed to do something fun that night, so I decided to treat the Lad and I to dinner at the Keg Mansion. It was my way of thanking him for being so attentive to Mom and the children.

The moment he was seated, he was chatting up the server, recalling his recent days in Ottawa before he made it to Toronto. Apparently he visited the Veterans Hospital in Ottawa wanting to pay a visit to soldiers mending from their injuries caused by their tour in Afghanistan. One of the things he did for his fellow mates was to order in dinner for all, from the Ottawa Keg. He had our server eating out of his hands. The Lad was beaming and suggested a round of drinks for the staff at the Keg. I quickly intervened and said that

Perfect Prey

was not possible. However, he could follow through on that gesture by creating a separate tab.

I assumed that the Lad would need a pep talk regarding next steps. I was wrong. He made it clear that he would land on his feet. In fact, he said that if he was abandoned on a street corner with little more than the clothes on his back, he would rebuild his existence and even improve on it within days.

The Irish Lad's wealth meant that work was only a means of making contacts. Such contacts would enable him to do the work he loved most. There was some confusion about what he loved to do most. *Let's see now, would that be opening a diner or corporate restructuring?*

While enjoying the food in front of us, the Irish Lad recalled his most recent venture in the restaurant business as the owner and principal cook for the Fish Café in Kerrisdale, B.C., 65-seats. Serving fresh seafood was the perfect balance between work and play.

Our plans were expanding before my eyes. The Irish Lad wanted us to keep an eye out for commercial properties suited to his diner dream. He imagined this venture to be a family affair; one that would employ and entertain us all.

I have begun to dance to his tune; it's just easier that way. I even suggested we name the diner, "Over the Hill." He loved it.

I e-mailed Mr. Date.Ca today and told him a half-truth. I said that the energy needed to cope with my divorce, care for Mom, the children, and my faltering business was pushing me to the limit. I did not tell him that I was being launched toward a church altar by a 270-pound cannon.

Then again, he had also told me a half-truth about his marital status. Sadly two halves equalled a whole lot of pain.

Karma will find me.

Tuesday, February 20, 2007

The Lad called me first thing to let me know that the Ontario Energy Savings Board hired him to perform similar duties. The only significant difference was the location. He would have to travel to Toronto's west end. It's funny how my first thought was that there is no honour among thieves – referring to the energy reselling business, of course.

Friday, March 2, 2007

Mom spent the day resting in her bed. I had hoped that today's Sweet 16 party for Tess would keep her mind off her knee. Of course, the Irish Lad's doting charm and vision for all of our future helped to fill the gaps.

Where did the time go?

Mom was a vision tonight. Her hair, make-up, nails all perfect. The royal blue dress and matching shoes combined to transform my baby into a woman. Seeing her smile made everything possible.

If only for a moment, my circumstances no longer defined me. I was the Mother of that beautiful, tall drink of water. I was the person who delivered on a promise to make magic: 14 formally dressed teenagers dining in Mom's home followed by a tour of Toronto in a stretch limo.

My friend Sarah and the Irish Lad functioned as servers. When the gang left for the limo they also helped me tidy up. The Irish Lad's gift was a promise to pay for coloured contact lenses and a $500 mall gift certificate.

Tess's Father had flown in from California to help her celebrate the balance of this monumental event. You can imagine the stress. I asked Tess not to mention the Irish Lad to her Father. She complied. I wanted to be the one to let him know that his children were within reach of *Happily Ever After*. I wanted to be the one to draft a letter to Lawzilla and tell her and her client to go to Hell.

Monday, March 5, 2007

Tess met with the optometrist today. My brown-eyed girl is now able bat her baby blues and tropical greens.

Rather than wait for the Lad to advance Tess the money for the appointment and prescription, I paid, fully expecting to be reimbursed by the Irish Lad.

The Irish Lad arrived at Mom's early that evening, without the money or the gift certificate, citing cash flow problems. I demanded he tell Tess that her "spending spree" at the mall was on hold. He did tell her but added an incentive for her demonstration of patience and maturity.

I stepped in and stated that he should not make promises that he cannot keep; particularly to children. He suggested that I not stress over such small matters given the bounty that awaited us all.

I took him aside and asked him to define "cash flow problems." This seemed completely absurd to me. Try not being able to buy food for your children.

It turns out that his commission cheque from Universal Energy bounced leaving him without "walking around" money. He had anticipated at least $4,000 and was fairly certain the Company stiffed him.

In response, I asked him why he didn't withdraw funds from his account in the face of this situation. He suggested that his organizational skills were in need of repair and that when money is always available you don't think about the possibility of being without it. *Try telling my 16-year-old that advice when she walks through the mall empty handed.* I am furious with myself for not being financially independent. The Irish Lad's promises are all I have to hang on to until Mom's knee heals and I can return to my business, full throttle.

Wednesday, March 7, 2007

The Irish Lad dropped over to let me know that he had arranged a custom-dress-designing appointment for me at Holt Renfrew for the beginning of April. The

The Irish Lad arrived at Mom's early that evening, without the money or the gift certificate, citing cash flow problems. I demanded he tell Tess that her "spending spree" at the mall was on hold. He did tell her but added an incentive for her demonstration of patience and maturity.

I stepped in and stated that he should not make promises that he cannot keep; particularly to children. He suggested that I not stress over such small matters given the bounty that awaited us all.

I took him aside and asked him to define "cash flow problems." This seemed completely absurd to me. Try not being able to buy food for your children.

It turns out that his commission cheque from Universal Energy bounced leaving him without "walking around" money. He had anticipated at least $4,000 and was fairly certain the Company stiffed him.

In response, I asked him why he didn't withdraw funds from his account in the face of this situation. He suggested that his organizational skills were in need of repair and that when money is always available you don't think about the possibility of being without it. *Try telling my 16-year-old that advice when she walks through the mall empty handed.* I am furious with myself for not being financially independent. The Irish Lad's promises are all I have to hang on to until Mom's knee heals and I can return to my business, full throttle.

Wednesday, March 7, 2007

The Irish Lad dropped over to let me know that he had arranged a custom-dress-designing appointment for me at Holt Renfrew for the beginning of April. The combined to transform my baby into a woman. Seeing her smile made everything possible.

If only for a moment, my circumstances no longer defined me. I was the Mother of that beautiful, tall drink of water. I was the person who delivered on a promise to make magic: 14 formally dressed teenagers dining in Mom's home followed by a tour of Toronto in a stretch limo.

My friend Sarah and the Irish Lad functioned as servers. When the gang left for the limo they also helped me tidy up. The Irish Lad's gift was a promise to pay for coloured contact lenses and a $500 mall gift certificate.

Tess's Father had flown in from California to help her celebrate the balance of this monumental event. You can imagine the stress. I asked Tess not to mention the Irish Lad to her Father. She complied. I wanted to be the one to let him know that his children were within reach of *Happily Ever After*. I wanted to be the one to draft a letter to Lawzilla and tell her and her client to go to Hell.

Monday, March 5, 2007

Tess met with the optometrist today. My brown-eyed girl is now able bat her baby blues and tropical greens.

Rather than wait for the Lad to advance Tess the money for the appointment and prescription, I paid, fully expecting to be reimbursed by the Irish Lad.

need for this dress was simple. The Weston family, specifically his close personal friend, Hilsey Weston was having a garden party in May and I needed to be prepared. This invitation was one of many needing a proper dress. He also suggested that I invite Sarah to join us at North 44 for the last Sunday in April to attend a gathering of his Rugby buddies, all of whom were professionals and, sometimes, single.

Instead of demanding details and contact information, I sat silent.

The search for a house became all-important. The clock was ticking and Dr. Siobhan Hill was making her way to Canada at the end of June. The Lad was frustrated, reminding me that his intention was to be out of the apartment by the end of March. Moreover, his terms for purchase would insist on a 30-day closing.

I have never spent this kind of money on a house before but have bought and sold enough properties to know that the Millar Team were the right people for the job. If I were to continue riding the Irish Lad's hamster wheel, I knew that having John as our purchasing agent would serve my need for laughter and keep my energy up. *Besides, he is edible.*

I made the introduction for the Irish Lad by telephone and our first meeting was set.

Saturday, March 10, 2007

As anticipated, John and the Irish Lad started off splendidly. Their love of boating, cars and "me" made for great chemistry.

John cracks me up. He is wickedly funny, politically incorrect and one of the sexiest men I have ever met. This is not a problem. I don't do married men. *Come to think of it, the Irish Lad is not funny.*

The Irish Lad kept us all busy, madly running between two homes. The first, a brand new construction located in the Hoggs Hollow listed at $2.6 million. A masterpiece, to say the least, with marble everything, state of the art appliances, heated floors, a wine cellar and the list goes on. The other property, an established estate located near Bayview and York Mills was dated, and came in at a lower listing price of $2.4 million. This mansion featured an in-ground pool, five car garage and circular parking with overflow for all of the Lad's so-called friends and associates.

As any good agent would do, John attempted to nail down the Irish Lad's financing plans. It was one thing to play real estate, another to put your money where your mouth is. We had tied up John's time, and the Lad offered few clues other than for this price point everything had to be just perfect.

John was able to get the Lad to commit to the following: He wanted a 30 day closing. *I want a 30 day divorce.* He would present a draft or certified cheque for $100,000 with an offer. He would not require a mortgage. *Great, then pay my Mastercard off!* He would prefer to have live-in staff. *You might want a personal trainer too.*

I may not be in real estate, but can appreciate the beauty of these terms.

Between the shuffle, we managed to test drive Land Rovers, Mercedes, and, God help me, *Bentleys*. The Grand Touring Land Rover/Bentley dealership located near Davenport and Dupont became a second home. I wanted to crawl under the salesman's desk when the Lad blurted out that he came by his money the old fashioned way, meaning he inherited it. Cringe.

When Isaac, the salesman, asked the Lad and I for our driver's license for verification prior to consenting to a test drive, I had noted the address on the Lad's was in Ottawa. My recollection was that he had traveled to Montreal, acquired the Ford Escape and passed through Ottawa only as a visitor.

We returned to the Estate located at Bayview and York Mills and met with John for one more round of "what's not quite right with this house." This time it was the snow. Significant ground cover made it difficult for the Lad to assess the grade and slope of the land. In addition, there was no way to assess the condition of the swimming pool. John reminded the Irish Lad that a top drawer inspection company could easily determine what, if any, issues existed with this home. He also suggested that for this price point he may want to invest as little as $5,000 for a pre-inspection to eliminate any guess-work.

To break the tension, John offered up a joke or two that offended the Irish Lad.

Tuesday, March 12, 2007

Tonight was a bloody circus. While seated at the dinner table, the Lad made it clear that he would not continue to work with John. He really over-reacted and there was no consoling him. He actually asked me to become involved in a good cop/bad cop routine that would result in having John fired as our agent. I refused to be part of this plan as the agent was a good friend and the Irish Lad's reaction was over the top. He excused himself from Mom's table and went home in a snit. He needed time to think. He needed time to think about my loyalty. This was the first time I had ever experienced him lost for words. The silence was golden.

The Irish Lad called to tell me that the deed was done. John was out and from now on we would be working directly with Karen and Ian. He also informed me that my disloyalty had forced him to rethink his plans to travel with me to Collingwood.

I said that traveling alone was perfectly acceptable to me, as was ending our relationship. He calmed down and suggested that we needed the time away if for no other reason that to collect our thoughts and step away from the maddening pace we had embarked on. *We?*

Thursday, March 15, 2007

The Irish Lad arrived a little later than expected at Mom's placing us in major northbound traffic. His delay was the result of his confusion about the bank's operating hours. He does not have a debit card and planned to visit the teller.

With Rachel in the backseat of his Ford Escape, we headed to Horseshoe Valley. Paul and Mary had invited Rachel to be their daughter's guest at the chalet. I have to admit the ride was filled with laughter and song. We had a ball. The mood was so positive that I could barely remember that 48 hours ago he fired the real estate agent. I said *barely*.

With many miles of skiing under his belt, between Whistler and the Alps, the Irish Lad took one look at the bumps at Horseshoe Valley and began to laugh. He marvelled at how we Ontarians would pay such extravagant lift ticket and membership fees for the benefit of skiing in 30-second increments. Try skiing on ice and then tell me how long 30 seconds feels.

The conversation between Paul and the Irish Lad was one way. Even a blind man could see that when the Lad has the floor there is little hope of anyone getting a word in edgewise. I have learned to sit back and let him have his moment. Bullshit, I sit still and drink wine.

The Irish Lad concluded his tour of all things self-promoting with an announcement. Paul, Mary and I all learned that our wedding was slated for June while the honeymoon was scheduled for mid-August.

Perfect Prey

With our mouths hanging wide open, he went on to tell us that while in Ireland, he planned to file adoption papers to grant Tess and Rachel international passports. The Lad saw the concern in our faces and he quickly assured us that this "gesture" was a means to an end. It would give Tess and Rachel European citizenship status making it possible for them to live and work anywhere in Europe. He hadn't asked for my permission. I was incensed. I looked stupid.

Knowing full well that there was a time and a place for everything, I managed to shift the conversation to Paul, highlighting his studies in England. Again, the Lad reclaimed the floor by asking Paul if he was fond of the water. I felt like saying why? *He flies to England – he doesn't swim across the Atlantic.*

The point was to allow the Irish Lad to make reference to his love of sailing his new 41-foot sailing yacht, soon to be moored in the Royal Canadian Yacht Club. Clearly the Lad is putting out a weekly newsletter and I am not on the mailing list. This was news to me.

Rather than endure one more announcement, I suggested we make our way to Collingwood.

Friday, March 16, 2007

In the bright light of day, the Irish Lad gave the place the once-over. He agreed that it was special and judging by my relaxed state insisted that I allow him to buy out my Husband. Then he would in turn gift that portion back to me for my own security. I was overwhelmed and began to look at this beautiful 1,219-square-foot Collingwood oasis as something of lasting value and a retreat from the maddening crowds.

There was unfinished business to discuss. The Lad had announced our wedding without my consent. We were not engaged, and I was not officially divorced. He glossed over the facts, stating that he was quite confident that my divorce was moments away.

True enough, but what does that have to do with the price of coffee in Columbia?

He wanted to marry me and that was that. He wanted to set June 15 as the date for two reasons: The arrival of his daughter and her ability to participate; and, to strike out at my ex-Husband using the irony of the date as a reminder of what can be accomplished in two short years following the total devastation of a family.

In the face of potentially good news, I remained down. He saw that and attempted to execute damage control. Showing flexibility and tolerance, he contacted the real estate agency where John worked and re-engaged the Team's services. The condition was that John remains a friend and that we work directly with Karen. It was a concession that won him points.

Back in the house-hunting game, the Toronto agent directed our attention to a few ideal properties and began to set up appointments for Sunday, March 18.

We hosted my dear friend, Suki for dinner and the evening. The Irish Lad never let her get a word in edgewise as he detailed his entire life story. Suki placed a few key comments that would size up his knowledge of skiing, mountain ranges as well as sailing. She was extremely knowledgeable about both, and, I gather, opted to defer her observations and opinions for a later time.

During her visit, I received a telephone call on my cell. The phone was beside the Irish Lad and rather than pass it over to me he answered. I instantly took offence, but contained my reaction. He did not ask for permission to answer my phone, nor had I asked him to intercept for the sake of convenience. I felt violated and knew this reaction was over the top given that this man was planning to marry me.

Mr. Law and Order was on the line. I went to my bedroom to have a private conversation. Our plan was to get together for coffee soon. Knowing that I was dating another man, Mr. Law and Order continued to keep tabs on me. I did not take this lightly. He has displayed genuine consideration for our friendship. Better late than never.

I returned to the living room and announced that the call was from my dear friend at the Ontario Provincial Police just checking in with me to see how I was doing.

Saturday, March 17, 2007

St. Patrick's Day morning came early. We had to pick up Rachel and head back to Toronto. The Irish Lad was not a fan of St. Paddy's claiming it had no real meaning for the Irish. It was a North American celebration lending itself to immigrant Irish in America or people needing a reason to get drunk. Again, he referenced his disgust with drinking and the people who drank to excess.

It was a long drive home. Rachel was about to commence the second week of her March Break while I faced work, countless errands, caring for Mom, the Lad's house hunt, search for a car, and now a wedding. There was also that small matter of returning to Court.

With little regard for how things work in my life, the Irish Lad burst through the front door and announced our wedding date. A celebration was in order, one that required the best of everything. He suggested we make a quick turn about and head for the market.

He must have had amnesia because he still had no money and I had no intentions of bankrolling this feast. Dinner had to be based on the groceries at hand, and I made that very clear. I reminded him that this would serve as a test of his expert chef skills. I did manage to rustle up sufficient funds to buy myself a bottle of wine.

Mom's recovery is going slower than expected. The pain in her knee is considerable and unresponsive to medication. It's her battle with nausea that doesn't make sense. Her sleep is poor as well. I wondered if it was her body withdrawing from the potent pain management.

The Lad and I sat with Mom in the living room and talked about this so-called wedding date. Mom's concern was simple. I was not divorced.

Sitting with my arms crossed on Mom's love seat, I began to experience anxiety like never before. I had agreed to marry a man who had yet to follow through or prove anything of value and yet, I no longer cared. Somehow marrying this man seemed the lesser of two evils. Without him I had been assured seemingly endless hardship at the hand of my Husband and lawyer. With him there was a chance that maybe I could leverage a little control and change the balance of power in the courtroom and in life.

Mom was very interested to learn about where we planned to get married. The Lad asked her where she wanted us to get married and she replied, Leaside United Church. Nobody asked the bride. Nor did I care.

We began to divide up responsibilities. Mom would make the introduction for the Lad and I to the minister, Ralph Taylor. My role was to rally the girls and focus on pretty things. The Lad was determined to manage all things related to the pomp and circumstance of the ceremony through to the details and location of the reception.

Then the announcement: He wanted our reception, indeed marriage to take place in our new home. This meant our house hunt would go into overdrive.

Realistically we had to be in our new home by June 1st. The two extraordinary properties already visited were equally ideal. The Lad placed Karen Millar on standby to receive our offer.

Karen, in response suggested he move on this immediately. The Irish Lad was not going to be pressured to make an offer without going over the pros and cons of each property to the point of total exhaustion.

Reams of paper all used for the creation of charts outlining costs and benefits kept us up for several nights.

The Lad would exaggerate the smallest and manageable problems and find fault with the way real estate was conducted in Ontario, indeed Canada.

Monday, March 19, 2007

Karen is a top producer because she knows that money talks and bullshit walks. She smelled a large pile. Given this, she invited me over to her home for a little wine, cheese and reality check. Her Husband, Ian, also in attendance, bottom-lined me. They sensed trouble and they wanted to know if I had any reason to believe that he was not what he claimed to be.

I could not answer them with 100 per cent assurance. I did attempt to communicate my belief in his genuineness. I tried to help them see the world through his eyes. I was their friend, and they wanted to protect me. To accept this protection would snuff out any chance of me rising above the pain and debt created by my Husband. They had succeeded in planting a seed of doubt.

Later that night I met with the Irish Lad and he could spot my frustration a mile away. Right out of the gate I stated we had found two ideal homes. They were both acceptable from the standpoint of price and location. Yet he continued to hesitate. I reminded him that if there was to be a wedding in either of these homes, the decision was now.

In response he calmly replied: "We must separate church and state. We will find our home on our terms. In the meantime I will investigate the availability of both the Four Seasons and the Park Hyatt in Yorkville. The in-house wedding planner and catering manager will handle the larger details and this will lighten your load."

Secretly, I had always dreamed of a wedding on the Sunnybrook Estate grounds, specifically, the Vaughan Estate. I called them and to my delight found our date to be available. I shared this joyous news with the Irish Lad. He responded by saying the Bride should have her day in her own way.

Once more, the Irish Lad found the Vaughan Estate to be reminiscent of his Father's home in Cobh, Ireland.

I had almost forgotten that we had left Karen Millar on standby.

any chance of me rising above the pain and debt created by my Husband. They had succeeded in planting a seed of doubt.

Later that night I met with the Irish Lad and he could spot my frustration a mile away. Right out of the gate I stated we had found two ideal homes. They were both acceptable from the standpoint of price and location. Yet he continued to hesitate. I reminded him that if there was to be a wedding in either of these homes, the decision was now.

In response he calmly replied: "We must separate church and state. We will find our home on our terms. In the meantime I will investigate the availability of both the Four Seasons and the Park Hyatt in Yorkville. The in-house wedding planner and catering manager will handle the larger details and this will lighten your load."

Secretly, I had always dreamed of a wedding on the Sunnybrook Estate grounds, specifically, the Vaughan Estate. I called them and to my delight found our date to be available. I shared this joyous news with the Irish Lad. He responded by saying the Bride should have her day in her own way.

Once more, the Irish Lad found the Vaughan Estate to be reminiscent of his Father's home in Cobh, Ireland.

I had almost forgotten that we had left Karen Millar on standby.

Realistically we had to be in our new home by June 1st. The two extraordinary properties already visited were equally ideal. The Lad placed Karen Millar on standby to receive our offer.

Karen, in response suggested he move on this immediately. The Irish Lad was not going to be pressured to make an offer without going over the pros and cons of each property to the point of total exhaustion.

Reams of paper all used for the creation of charts outlining costs and benefits kept us up for several nights.

The Lad would exaggerate the smallest and manageable problems and find fault with the way real estate was conducted in Ontario, indeed Canada.

Monday, March 19, 2007

Karen is a top producer because she knows that money talks and bullshit walks. She smelled a large pile. Given this, she invited me over to her home for a little wine, cheese and reality check. Her Husband, Ian, also in attendance, bottom-lined me. They sensed trouble and they wanted to know if I had any reason to believe that he was not what he claimed to be.

I could not answer them with 100 per cent assurance. I did attempt to communicate my belief in his genuineness. I tried to help them see the world through his eyes. I was their friend, and they wanted to protect me. To accept this protection would snuff out

Tuesday, March 20, 2007

Today began with purpose. In the background was the promise of my divorce decree being delivered while in the foreground the need to engage the services of my dear friend, Louise, as Matron of Honour.

My "to do" list was rapidly advancing, and I needed to source a photographer, confirm the minister and the reception facility. It was my hope that Louise would accept and as such, guide me directly to gown retailers, florists and invitation houses. Louise accepted and called on her countless resources on file as only she could to place me on the right path.

The Lad had specifically asked to handle all things edible including his fascination with ice sculptures.

The wheels were in motion and the pace tripled. The Vaughan Estate's catering manager e-mailed a contract to my attention for our June 15th nuptials. The deposit required was $1,495.00.

Mom was bound and determined to be up and walking well for the wedding. I am still very concerned about her struggles with nausea, extreme pain, and sleeplessness.

Following dinner, I called Irish Lad John to ask him for his daughter's e-mail address. It was time to make some kind of introduction and suggest we begin corresponding to learn more about each other.

John was delighted by my enthusiasm to reach out, and offered this address: shill@campus.ie.

My letter to Siobhan went as follows:

Hello Siobhan.

I hope you don't mind me taking this opportunity to reach out and say hello.

I am quite certain your Dad has shared a few key details about my rather complicated life complete with one-eyed Yorkie, two daughters possessed by Barbie's values and of course, the fact that I live with my 72 year old Mom.

The grim details that lead me back to my Mom's doorstep are conversation for another day. At this time, I'd rather just keep our communication simple.

It has come to my attention that together we may possess the power to keep John spinning in the wind. I am fairly effective at teasing and tormenting your Dad, but recognize that there is strength in numbers. Your arrival in Toronto is highly desired. Think of us as running a four woman relay where you, I, Tess and Rachel each have the opportunity to pass the baton and take a turn at keeping John off balance. Truly, I believe that this is God's divine plan.

I am not going to detail how wonderful your Father is because I know you have greater expertise in this area. I am going to tell you that John has entered our lives in a category six tornado and we are still waiting for the dust to settle. In the meantime I take great pleasure in spending time getting to know him.

Perfect Prey

He may have shared with you that I am self-employed as a corporate health promotion or wellness consultant. In short, I facilitate health risk prevention education for employees. My team of experts comprises dieticians, physiotherapists, kinesiologists, registered nurses, chiropodists, optometrists, massage therapists, etc. And yes, for the record, I am all over your Dad to get up and start walking.

Family stats include: Tess 16 (March 2, 1991), Rachel 13 (December 31, 1993) and me, August 5, 1962. In common all three of us have brown eyes, varying shades of blonde and light brown hair and height, lots of height. I tip the measuring tape at 5'11", Tess 5'9" and Rachel 5'6". Your Dad claims to be 6' but I am highly suspicious.

Oops, Kobe is eight pounds and was born on June 11, 2002.

Please feel free to contact me.
If you wish to take peaks at my website check out www.workingatwellness.com.

I have attached some snaps of the four of us.

Be well and thank you for receiving this greeting.

Affectionately, Liz Cole

Perfect Prey

Saturday, March 24, 2007

Real estate remained a high priority for the Lad. In addition to revisiting the top two choices, again, a third property was brought to our attention. This selection was exquisite, below the price points of the other two homes, new construction, impeccable details, and first rate building materials. Close to Avenue Road and Lawrence, the location was brilliant.

Ian Millar was on deck for today's tour. His role on the Millar Team was to assist clients with understanding the physical benefits and limitations of any property. After a significant interior and exterior inspection of the premise, he was unable to identify any faults associated with this listing. He had even learned that the closing date may fall well within our extreme deadline. The only problem was that the owners were in Australia and not accepting offers until Wednesday, March 28th. The terms were a tad off-putting, but offered the Lad time to organize his financing and to take one final look at houses number one and two for comparison.

There was time amidst the chaos to return to Mom's, check in on her needs and give the dog a break. Mom was keeper of the real estate listings. The colourful expensively laid out brochures were always within arms reach. Visitors to Mom's house were all encouraged to peruse the magnificent listing brochures. Would the Lad and Liz pick Door Number One, Two or Three?

We spent the entire afternoon test driving cars. I began with Mercedes and noticed my level of comfort increasing while my feelings of inadequacy lessening. God help me I have become open to the idea of living well.

Minutes before midnight, the Lad and I began to have a very intense and disturbing conversation about his need for me to have his child. I do not want more children as I could not assure their safe and healthy arrival into this world. At the age of 45 it was my belief that the risks outweighed the benefits. Besides, I am done. I love being a Mother to adolescent aged children. I love the increasing freedom that came with their independence.

The Lad became very quiet. It begged the question, do you want another child? He said: "I always have since the loss of my son, Andrew."

This was the first mention of a second child. In a matter of seconds he revealed that while living in Vancouver, a drunk driver killed his four-year-old son. He also felt that the pain and suffering that resulted from this tragedy ultimately caused the failure of his marriage.

In the face of this information, I could only offer my most heartfelt sympathy and credit him for doing such a wonderful job as Siobhan's parent.

Sunday, March 25, 2007

It was cocktail hour at Mom's and the grand dame was holding court. The Lad and I flew in with the intentions of debriefing about everything. We had houses and automobiles to flow chart and run a cost/benefit analysis. This would have to wait as Mom had guests and the Lad had a new audience.

On the far wall, seated in the loveseat was Auntie Peggy, a lifetime friend and Dubliner. In the corner sat Stewart, our next door neighbour and silent observer. In the other corner sat Kerry, a woman of great substance, life experience and years. The lights were about to dim and the curtains about to open. The Lad had fresh ears.

What he didn't anticipate was the need to flex his use of Gaelic. It was time for the Lad to live up to one of his dating profile claims of being multi-lingual. On record he spoke French, Gaelic, a little Russian, Yiddish *and Bullshit*.

The banter in Gaelic between Auntie Peggy and the Lad seemed superficial comprising basic salutations. However, sufficient words were spoken to keep us all engaged in the possibility that he did in fact speak Gaelic.

Then the bomb dropped. The Irish Lad mentioned the wedding. Mom nearly imploded. This was not kosher. There was to be a time and place for such an announcement and the Lad blew it. Mom was visibly angered while the group sat in silence struggling to dodge the elephant in the living room.

I gave the Lad an elbow to the ribs and uttered: "Be quiet." He didn't understand. Why would he. The world always revolved around him.

More to the point, my highly anticipated divorce decree had not made its way into my lawyer's hands. Talk of marriage was completely inappropriate.

As always the ground beneath my feet was shifting. I had assumed that tonight might end on a quiet note. Instead, the Lad received a call from Karen Millar. The vendors for property number three wanted to deal. They had news of our interest and were smart enough to seize the moment.

I was shaking. It was show time and the plan was for the Lad to meet Karen in her office mid day tomorrow to sign an offer and provide a deposit for $100,000. I had not anticipated the Lad's reaction.

Out of nowhere was this rage. The Lad was incensed and felt manipulated by the vendor's agent as well as Karen. He was not going to be railroaded into making any deals with anyone outside his own terms. If we were to lose this property then so be it, otherwise the deal would go down on Wednesday as previously discussed. The Lad's intense business schedule for Monday and Tuesday had been previously determined and there was no opportunity for him to attend to any banking.

I did suggest that 99 per cent of the banking could be transacted over the telephone resulting only in his signature being required. He would not hear of it and commenced sulking. He accused me of being part of the Millar Team rather than on his team.

Karen attempted to calm him down and suggested that she would draw up an offer dated for Wednesday in an effort to save time. He complied.

Monday, March 26, 2007

The urgency of everything surrounds me.

I called Mr. $375.00 an Hour to establish the whereabouts of my decree. His assistant made the call downtown to the Courthouse and was told that it had been processed and was seconds away from being dispatched. It was a done deal.

Seconds later Karen Millar called me to tell me that the house deal was off. A competitive offer was accepted by the vendors. I suggested she call the Lad with the news. She did.

He was furious. He suggested that his insinuation of being manipulated was affirmed. He could trust no one in the Canadian real estate market. Any future deal would be private.

With that news, I forged ahead and made contact with a local photographer and scheduled a meeting for 5:30 P.M.

I felt an instant connection with Donna Miller. Her studio was eclectic and cozy. By contrast, the Irish

Perfect Prey

Lad used the studio as a stage to perform his usual rant about his wealth. It was bizarre. He had not allowed Donna the chance to communicate her experiences as a wedding photographer, nor had he even gestured to look at her work. Instead he boasted that whatever the result, he would need multiple copies of the wedding album for his family abroad. He also insisted that we book a sitting for our family portrait.

I have learned to tune him out and I busied myself with her albums. It was clear that Donna and the Irish Lad were not on the same page, and I needed to help them connect. I drew the Lad's attention to a photograph of a massive sailboat on the wall. Alas, the photographer was a sailor. Once again, we were sidetracked by the Lad's talk of racing and club memberships.

He had not so much as looked at one sample wedding album when he blurted out an offer of employment to Donna followed with an invitation to her family to attend the wedding. The gesture would not have been complete without a second, more important invitation for Donna and family to join us on his boat at the Royal Canadian Yacht Club for a sail in July.

We parted with a clear understanding that she had the job and that a deposit of 50 per cent ($1,500.00) was required. The Irish Lad asked her if she would dodge the tax man if he paid her in cash.

He then went on to confirm that he would drop in on Thursday with the money and sign the contract.

Tuesday, March 27, 2007

Siobhan emailed me back today and included a photograph. My family's reaction to her was similar. She appeared awfully young for a 25 year old woman. We mentioned our reaction to the Lad and he took full credit for her youthful genes.

Her letter read:

Hiya Liz:

Congratulations on the relationship and your wedding. I am so happy for the two of you. Thanks for taking the first step by writing me; I was a little nervous about writing you before we met. This is a big step for all of us. I am looking forward to meeting you and your family. I always wanted sisters. I feel that this is a good thing for all of us.

Dad can seem a bit scatter brained, but don't be fooled by his approach to things. He always has his fingers in more pots than he seems to be able to handle. But in the end he pulls off a miracle and everything gets done. So that just seems like a tornado to some. I am used to it, but I enjoy seeing the effect that it has on some.

Anything to get Dad off balance is good. From your letter you must be keeping him off balance. Be aware that he can have a strong need to get back with practical jokes when pushed. Most tend to involve water and getting wet. Good Luck.

Tell Tess and Rachel that I would be happy to hear from them. I can't wait to meet all of you. I should be in Toronto by June 25 at the latest.

My flatmate took this pic tonight so you can see what I look like going through my boards, stressed? I promise to write after the Boards are over.

Love Siobhan, "whatever you do, do no harm."

Wednesday, March 28, 2007

In the face of so much change remains the unfinished business with my Husband. I should be able to refer to him as my ex-Husband but the decree has gone missing.

Tomorrow is all about being in Court. The two month deferral granted to my Husband was done. Motions for child support, retroactive money owed and commitment on shared expenses associated with the condo and storage fees were top priorities.

On the other side of the looking-glass, wedding plans marched on as follows:

Meet with Minister from Leaside United Church at 6:00 P.M. on March 29th.
Meet with the Catering Director at the Vaughan Estate at Noon on March 31st.
Revisit House One as it is a private listing on March 31st.
Test-drive Land Rover again on March 31st.
Confirm that I will be divorced before I remarry.

I had not anticipated a visit from the Lad. I did not want one. Yet he appeared, only this time dressed to the nines in his kilt, Prince Albert jacket, brogues, sporran and yes, regimental. He was a vision. Mom and I were suitably impressed and entertained.

He only stayed 15 minutes. Perhaps he finally had noticed that less is more.

Thursday, March 29, 2007

I was going to court with a certain spring in my step. Mr. $375.00 an Hour, his legal associate Ms. Even Keel and I had prepared every last court required document. We always had. It was also Mr. $375.00 an Hour's birthday and I had prepared brownies.

Team Deferral headed up by Lawzilla had not produced the required financial disclosures, and I knew this because each team is required to advance documentation to each other prior to appearing in court. I was heading into court with confidence. I had the Luck of the Irish.

Mr. $375.00 an Hour noted the name of the Justice assigned to our courtroom. She was known as a straight shooter. She did not tolerate nonsense. We were number four out of five on the case list to be heard.

I sat in the back of the courtroom with Ms. Even Keel along with the other women awaiting justice. Dark under eye circles, sallow skin and clenched fists united us. Except for Ms. Even Keel. In her case God doled out the total package; brains, beauty and personality.

I had not anticipated a visit from the Lad. I did not want one. Yet he appeared, only this time dressed to the nines in his kilt, Prince Albert jacket, brogues, sporran and yes, regimental. He was a vision. Mom and I were suitably impressed and entertained.

He only stayed 15 minutes. Perhaps he finally had noticed that less is more.

Thursday, March 29, 2007

I was going to court with a certain spring in my step. Mr. $375.00 an Hour, his legal associate Ms. Even Keel and I had prepared every last court required document. We always had. It was also Mr. $375.00 an Hour's birthday and I had prepared brownies.

Team Deferral headed up by Lawzilla had not produced the required financial disclosures, and I knew this because each team is required to advance documentation to each other prior to appearing in court. I was heading into court with confidence. I had the Luck of the Irish.

Mr. $375.00 an Hour noted the name of the Justice assigned to our courtroom. She was known as a straight shooter. She did not tolerate nonsense. We were number four out of five on the case list to be heard.

I sat in the back of the courtroom with Ms. Even Keel along with the other women awaiting justice. Dark under eye circles, sallow skin and clenched fists united us. Except for Ms. Even Keel. In her case God doled out the total package; brains, beauty and personality.

Tell Tess and Rachel that I would be happy to hear from them. I can't wait to meet all of you. I should be in Toronto by June 25 at the latest.

My flatmate took this pic tonight so you can see what I look like going through my boards, stressed? I promise to write after the Boards are over.

Love Siobhan, "whatever you do, do no harm."

Wednesday, March 28, 2007

In the face of so much change remains the unfinished business with my Husband. I should be able to refer to him as my ex-Husband but the decree has gone missing.

Tomorrow is all about being in Court. The two month deferral granted to my Husband was done. Motions for child support, retroactive money owed and commitment on shared expenses associated with the condo and storage fees were top priorities.

On the other side of the looking-glass, wedding plans marched on as follows:

Meet with Minister from Leaside United Church at 6:00 P.M. on March 29th.
Meet with the Catering Director at the Vaughan Estate at Noon on March 31st.
Revisit House One as it is a private listing on March 31st.
Test-drive Land Rover again on March 31st.
Confirm that I will be divorced before I remarry.

The first three cases were heard in rapid succession. The women all faired well enough to give me hope. There were no slam dunks, just movement in the direction that protected children. My spirits continued to rise. It looked as though I was going to get out of the courtroom under budget with my lawyer's time and save $2.00 on parking.

When called, my lawyer spoke first. He was concise and to the point, making way for a speedy outcome. I never took my eyes off of Lawzilla. She was called to task. Rising from the depths of hell, Lawzilla gave Windsor Ontario's altar boy and MVP (back in the 1970s) a voice. Theatrical, unorganized and irrelevant, she managed to provoke the Justice. Driven to distraction, the Judge overlooked our sworn affidavits.
Weeks of preparation and financial expense were completely disregarded. The chaos created by Lawzilla caused the Justice to ignore our efforts and defer her ruling to a later date. This is how the law works. Team Deferral knew that in order to dodge the obvious, their ongoing failure to disclose financial documents, they needed to create a distraction and gain another deferral. The Justice refused to make any orders about my motions for support and called a recess. Her rulings would come at a later time. We were dismissed.

I had failed to do right by my children and their Father continued to do nothing with the blessing of the Ministry of the Attorney General.

I could barely breathe. I was no further ahead. I will be required to appear again at great personal expense.

Mr. $375.00 an Hour did not see this coming. He did see my face though and quickly suggested a much-needed field trip.

10th Floor Women's Clothing, Shoes and Martial Status

Leaning against a clerk's counter, Mr. $375.00 an Hour asked the young clerk to call up my file. He wanted to show me that I was in fact "divorced" and that seeing it on the computer screen might sufficiently distract me from the disappointment on the 9th floor.

Blank. The screen made no reference to having ever applied for my divorce.

He approached my file from every angle referencing my name, file number and choice of weapon. Blank.

I wanted to cry. I asked him what this all meant. The clerk stepped in and tried to offer a little reassurance saying that sometimes this happens and that she was sure it would turn up. Meanwhile think positive. Think positive is the government's way of saying expect us to mess things up, that's what we do best.

Thinking positive may take a little incentive: Let's review:

1. No orders issued in support of my children.
2. No divorce sworn by the Province of Ontario.
3. Reached the maximum parking expense of $18.
4. Still had to pay Mr. $375 an Hour for our half-day in court.

5. No financial relief for shared property expenses.
6. No time-out from being a 24/7 parent.
7. Sold my soul to the Devil by accepting the Lad's offer of marriage.

Meanwhile the Irish Lad was supposed to deliver the deposit to the photographer and we had a meeting with my Minister for 6:00 P.M. For reasons that did not impress me, the Irish Lad failed to make it to the bank and failed to deliver the deposit. I contacted the photographer to let her know that we would be in on Friday before 4:00 P.M.

We crossed the park in front of Mom's house. The Church was on the other side. *So much history associated with this Church for my family. Finally, I was to be married in my home parish.*

The banter between the Irish Lad and the Minister was rich. We filled out forms associated with the blessed event and agreed to take a marriage preparation course. I booked our course at a nearby church for Friday, April 13th. I paid $148.00 and didn't bat an eyelash. It seemed a fair concession given that the Irish Lad was buying us a mansion, paying for the wedding, buying the Collingwood condo, taking us to Europe and acquiring a luxury car for my use.

Nothing silences a pre-marriage meeting faster than telling a Minister that your divorce has not been officially granted. Ralph, experienced in the ways of all things miraculous did not flinch. He calmly said: "Keep me in the loop."

The reality of my future is setting in and keeping busy helps me to rationalize the sale of my soul.

Mr. Date.Ca, now a distant memory, continues to keep me warm at night. I still recall every detail of our dinner date at Mom's. I hope he is able to get his house in order some day and re-emerge in the dating world unencumbered. I wished he had done this the first time. Mr. Law and Order continues to work on getting us together for coffee and though I would enjoy the chance to catch up with him, time is scarce.

Friday, March 30, 2007

"I've been hit by a car," said the Irish Lad. Just after 10:30 A.M. the Irish Lad called me from his cell phone to tell me that he had been struck to the ground by a car while standing in his workplace parking lot. He was certain that he would be okay, but since the back of his head hit the pavement with some force, he wanted to have it checked out.

This news stopped me dead in my tracks. I care about his well-being and want to be at his side. His business associate was driving him to the hospital in the Ford Escape. I failed to ask for the name of the hospital. Knowing the location of his workplace, I assumed one of three possibilities: St. Joe's, Trillium on the Queensway and Etobicoke General. He did not want me at his side suggesting that the hospital visit would be in and out. The Irish Lad assured me he'd call. Then he reminded me that his cell phone would be turned off as per hospital rules.

By Noon I still had not heard a word from the Irish Lad. I began to call the emergency rooms of the three hospitals in search of the Irish Lad. My second call was to Trillium and the triage nurse confirmed that a man

Perfect Prey

fitting the Irish Lad's description and possible injury was on his way to the imaging department. She did not confirm his name. I gave her my cell number and asked her to tell the patient to call me.

I had the usual errands to run including taking Mom for her physiotherapy appointment. While seated in the car, I decided to call Mr. $375.00 an Hour in the hopes of hearing about the status of my divorce as well as to tell him of the Lad's injury.

The divorce remained missing in action. His concern for the Lad's wellbeing was touching. His concern for me is nothing short of receiving a gift with purchase.

While the Lad was employed by Universal Energy Corporation, Mr. $375.00 an Hour had his friend, the company's controller, provide feedback on the Lad. Basically, the Lad was liked and worked hard.

By 2:45 P.M., I had not heard from the Lad. I returned Mom to the comfort of her home and headed to Trillium Health Centre. I feel guilty about what was going through my mind. Here I was off to be at my future Husband's side and all I could think about was his promise to make it to the bank and produce certified cheques for the Vaughan Estate and the photographer.

I did not have total confirmation that he was at the Trillium, but headed there anyway. The plan was that I would suggest his business associate drive his car home while I drove the Irish Lad. Then I would give the business associate a lift home. It occurred to me that I did not even have the name of the business associate. Within 50 metres of the parking lot entrance, my cell rang and it was the Irish Lad, calling from home. I was furious and told him to stay put as I was on my way.

It was 4:30 P.M. and the Irish Lad made his way toward me in the usual fashion. Something was wrong. I did not mask my thoughts in a poker-face. His reaction was to over-act his confusion and short-term memory loss. He went as far as to almost faint then emerge as if in a disoriented state.

I was cool. I asked him what hospital he was admitted to and he replied Humber River. I said let me see your hospital bracelet so I can attend your follow-up appointment. He said that he discarded the annoying plastic wristlet on discharge. I responded by asking for the paperwork. Again, he came up empty.

I gave him a few seconds to look me in the eyes, and he did. It was like looking into the eyes of a reptile. I bluffed and said how curious it was that his admittance was confirmed at Trillium Health Centre, though it wasn't. He quickly adjusted his story to agree with mine. He reminded me that he was a stranger in a strange land.

I looked at the clock and it was 5:00 P.M. I asked to see the back of his head. On examination there was no sign of injury. Ticked off I suggested he grab his coat because we had less than one hour to get to his bank located way uptown. He fell back to a seated position and said that he could not manage the journey, but would on Monday.

My heart sank into my stomach and my head began to pound. I felt betrayed. There was no doubt in my mind that the Lad had not sustained a head injury. It rang and it was the Irish Lad, calling from home. I was furious and told him to stay put as I was on my way.

It was 4:30 P.M. and the Irish Lad made his way toward me in the usual fashion. Something was wrong. I did not mask my thoughts in a poker-face. His reaction was to over-act his confusion and short-term memory loss. He went as far as to almost faint then emerge as if in a disoriented state.

I was cool. I asked him what hospital he was admitted to and he replied Humber River. I said let me see your hospital bracelet so I can attend your follow-up appointment. He said that he discarded the annoying plastic wristlet on discharge. I responded by asking for the paperwork. Again, he came up empty.

I gave him a few seconds to look me in the eyes, and he did. It was like looking into the eyes of a reptile. I bluffed and said how curious it was that his admittance was confirmed at Trillium Health Centre, though it wasn't. He quickly adjusted his story to agree with mine. He reminded me that he was a stranger in a strange land.

I looked at the clock and it was 5:00 P.M. I asked to see the back of his head. On examination there was no sign of injury. Ticked off I suggested he grab his coat because we had less than one hour to get to his bank located way uptown. He fell back to a seated position and said that he could not manage the journey, but would on Monday.

My heart sank into my stomach and my head began to pound. I felt betrayed. There was no doubt in my mind that the Lad had not sustained a head injury. It fitting the Irish Lad's description and possible injury was on his way to the imaging department. She did not confirm his name. I gave her my cell number and asked her to tell the patient to call me.

I had the usual errands to run including taking Mom for her physiotherapy appointment. While seated in the car, I decided to call Mr. $375.00 an Hour in the hopes of hearing about the status of my divorce as well as to tell him of the Lad's injury.

The divorce remained missing in action. His concern for the Lad's wellbeing was touching. His concern for me is nothing short of receiving a gift with purchase.

While the Lad was employed by Universal Energy Corporation, Mr. $375.00 an Hour had his friend, the company's controller, provide feedback on the Lad. Basically, the Lad was liked and worked hard.

By 2:45 P.M., I had not heard from the Lad. I returned Mom to the comfort of her home and headed to Trillium Health Centre. I feel guilty about what was going through my mind. Here I was off to be at my future Husband's side and all I could think about was his promise to make it to the bank and produce certified cheques for the Vaughan Estate and the photographer.

I did not have total confirmation that he was at the Trillium, but headed there anyway. The plan was that I would suggest his business associate drive his car home while I drove the Irish Lad. Then I would give the business associate a lift home. It occurred to me that I did not even have the name of the business associate. Within 50 metres of the parking lot entrance, my cell was as if my feet were cemented to his floor while my mind raced out the door. Please God don't let this man be lying to me. I can't take more disappointment. I can't bear the humiliation of being the world's biggest doormat again. This was my lowest moment.

Frustrated, I called around to various wedding service providers and explained the circumstances surrounding our delay. In response they were empathetic. I needed them to refuse our business.

Mr. $375.00 an Hour called over to see how the Irish Lad was doing. Then he got to the point. He suggested that we postpone the wedding as a precaution. I was to reorder a copy of my marriage certificate on-line and was told the earliest date that I would be eligible to be married would be June 29th. Was this a sign?

The Irish Lad assumed that I was disappointed and offered a win-win solution. Move the wedding date to Friday, July 6th. This way he would have the best 50th birthday imaginable.

As if in automatic, I began to call wedding personnel including the Minister, the photographer and the Catering Manager at the Vaughan Estate if only to check availability.

As the Luck of the Irish would have it, all available.

Still over-acting about his so-called head injury, he suggested that we go out for dinner to take my mind off the disappointment of my divorce status. Ironically I was far more disappointed in myself for enduring the Lad's deceit. Then, as if on auto-pilot, I went out for dinner. He selected a chipper Irish Pub complete with entertainment. Within one hour he had managed to buy a round for the band and engage the services of the piper for our wedding.

I wasn't completely resigned to the events of the day. Though I agreed to stay over, I was in no way interested in being with him, at all. He tried to get into my good books by contacting the headquarters of Starbucks to order 150 gift cards as part of our wedding thank you gifts to be handed out at the Vaughan Estate. He suggested this item because that is where we first met.

I feel like a choking victim in a restaurant. *I know that my cough is annoying the other diners and I need help. Rather than ask for help and save my own life, I quietly slip away into the washroom and suffocate.*

Saturday, March 31, 2007

We visited with the Catering Director at the Vaughan Estate at noon today. The Irish Lad and the Catering Director are cut from the same cloth as they are both self-proclaimed "foodies." They talked about restaurants, fine food shops, and wine. I nodded and encouraged that we start the tour. I also pointed out that our booking had changed from the 15th of June to July 6th and explained why. The Catering Director said they could grant that change and would draw up a new contract, which could be completed and returned on Monday or Tuesday with our deposit.

Perfect Prey

It was late Saturday afternoon and everything was in process. Our next appointment was at Land Rover. I was to knuckle down and pick a model. I was to test drive this vehicle with an eye to owning it. I was to pick a colour and leather interior. I was to enjoy this moment.

I took the wheel of this magnificent vehicle. Isaac, the salesperson rode shotgun while the Lad rambled on from the back seat. The two men had made a connection based on their time residing in Montreal. Isaac's former life was in the garment industry with connections to bridal wear. The Lad referenced an old acquaintance by the name of Marty Lemish whom he worked with when in Vancouver, also of the rag trade. Isaac did not recognize this name. I continued to drive and marvel at the gadgets.

The Lad was fascinated by Toronto's Casa Loma. He never missed an opportunity to drive by this local treasure and ridicule it for being referred to as a castle. He went on to describe his family's Kensington House in London, now used as an income property left to his management. He said this massive residence was left to him by his Grandfather in lieu of a cash inheritance. As for the $50,000 forwarded to the Lad from a trust fund each year, well, he couldn't look a gift horse in the mouth.

It was a long and productive day. The Moody Blues were playing on the radio, and the Lad revealed that they were chums of both his Father and his Uncle. Exhausted, I suggested we cook and eat in. We ate and fell asleep, apart.

He approached the bed sometime around 2:00 A.M. in a manic state. It was as if he was three years old and wanted to play. This was not about sex; it was about being annoying. It was about the Lad wanting to stay up all night and talk about himself. I was not in the mood for such behaviour and told him. Then in a callous tone I said that I would rather sleep with my Husband than endure this ridiculous behaviour.

This levelled him. In a snit, he returned to the living room, put on his clothes and went for a drive. He returned around 5:30 A.M. with every newspaper conceivable. Tired, I remained tucked in the bed until 7:30 A.M. Unimpressed by his sulking, I turned on Coronation Street and enjoyed the program.

Sunday, April 1, 2007

By 9:00 A.M. this spoiled brat realized that he had not achieved the desired result. He changed tactics and told me that my comment about preferring my Husband's company to his struck a fatal blow to his heart and affection for me.

Under-whelmed by his damaged state, I suggested he not act like such an idiot moving forward. Also, I was no longer available to hunt real estate or cars. He was on his own as my time was at a premium. I would gladly approve of any choices he made.

I hit the shower, and together we picked up Rachel and her theatre buddies and drove them to class. Back on the road I suggested a visit to Bayview Village Shopping Mall where I could complete an errand at the Chapter's store. I left the Lad thumbing through sailing

Perfect Prey

magazines. From there we made our way into Restoration Hardware, an upscale home decor store. Within five minutes, he began laying out an order for delivery. He had fallen in love with a bedroom suite, linens, leather furniture and so on. I reminded him that an address was required first. The salesperson remarked that an address would help as would a deposit.

I walked away.

Moments later I was standing in front of the diamond ring display case at a nearby jewellery store. I had tried on diamond rings from time to time all valued around $12,000. They were all exceptional in their craftsmanship and yet I never accepted the offer to possess one. The ring being presented for my consideration was valued at $36,000. The Lad spoke the language of carats, colour, cut, class and source. I could barely breathe, but remained calm and indicated my pleasure with the ring on my finger. I also made it clear that with our wedding date confirmed for July 6th I would now accept his ring.

He took me aside and said he had a "cousin" in the business that could produce a higher grade of diamond for about the same money.

I walked away.

We went to a culinary arts store and looked at high-end chef's knives. He was, without exception, the most annoying customer that store had ever experienced. He made the salesperson take out one knife after another and then performed as if at a Japanese cooking table.

I walked away.

While in Chapters I bought a Bride's Magazine. The table had turned. Now I was going to start cutting out pictures of beautiful dresses, rings, all things bridal and barrage the Irish Lad with a symphony of wedding bells. I even asked him to consider releasing butterflies at the blessed event.

We headed back downtown and collected the girls. Once we had them back in their respective homes, I reminded the Irish Lad that we had to grocery shop for the evening meal. It was he that got me in the habit of shopping for our daily bread as the Europeans do!

I had changed the way I behaved, and the Irish Lad was agitated as if overdue for medication. His menu suggestions were over-the-top and not in keeping with what my children would eat. He took offence and removed himself from the equation suggesting we go our separate ways this evening. He reminded me that it was hard for him to walk among the lower classes and do as they do. He tired of the common way we approached food and in particular our thirst for alcohol.

Note to self: Make mine a double.

Monday, April 2, 2007

The Catering Manager from the Vaughan Estate, and the photographer called. It was go time. Deposits and contracts needed to be completed. The Irish Lad was too busy with client meetings to attend to the required banking. He asked me once again to call the photographer and the Vaughan Estate to make the necessary apologies for the delay.

While in Chapters I bought a Bride's Magazine. The table had turned. Now I was going to start cutting out pictures of beautiful dresses, rings, all things bridal and barrage the Irish Lad with a symphony of wedding bells. I even asked him to consider releasing butterflies at the blessed event.

We headed back downtown and collected the girls. Once we had them back in their respective homes, I reminded the Irish Lad that we had to grocery shop for the evening meal. It was he that got me in the habit of shopping for our daily bread as the Europeans do!

I had changed the way I behaved, and the Irish Lad was agitated as if overdue for medication. His menu suggestions were over-the-top and not in keeping with what my children would eat. He took offence and removed himself from the equation suggesting we go our separate ways this evening. He reminded me that it was hard for him to walk among the lower classes and do as they do. He tired of the common way we approached food and in particular our thirst for alcohol.

Note to self: Make mine a double.

Monday, April 2, 2007

The Catering Manager from the Vaughan Estate, and the photographer called. It was go time. Deposits and contracts needed to be completed. The Irish Lad was too busy with client meetings to attend to the required banking. He asked me once again to call the photographer and the Vaughan Estate to make the necessary apologies for the delay.

magazines. From there we made our way into Restoration Hardware, an upscale home decor store. Within five minutes, he began laying out an order for delivery. He had fallen in love with a bedroom suite, linens, leather furniture and so on. I reminded him that an address was required first. The salesperson remarked that an address would help as would a deposit.

I walked away.

Moments later I was standing in front of the diamond ring display case at a nearby jewellery store. I had tried on diamond rings from time to time all valued around $12,000. They were all exceptional in their craftsmanship and yet I never accepted the offer to possess one. The ring being presented for my consideration was valued at $36,000. The Lad spoke the language of carats, colour, cut, class and source. I could barely breathe, but remained calm and indicated my pleasure with the ring on my finger. I also made it clear that with our wedding date confirmed for July 6th I would now accept his ring.

He took me aside and said he had a "cousin" in the business that could produce a higher grade of diamond for about the same money.

I walked away.

We went to a culinary arts store and looked at high-end chef's knives. He was, without exception, the most annoying customer that store had ever experienced. He made the salesperson take out one knife after another and then performed as if at a Japanese cooking table.

I walked away.

Perfect Prey

Something nudged me toward calling my lawyer first. They found my divorce. In an effort to keep the Lad off balance, I called him and said that June 15th was back on. I also let him know that I had called the Minister, catering manager and photographer and they were all available. There could be no delays regarding deposits.

He was thrilled to learn that we could be married as originally planned. He apologized for being financially irresponsible. In turn, I said that I would place the Vaughan Estate deposit on my MasterCard and sign his name to the contract for the balance. He agreed to this.

In preparation for a major business event scheduled for Tuesday, April 3rd, I went to the grocery store to buy supplies for a nutrition display. My cell phone rang and it was the Minister. He could not reach my Mom but did see a large amount of emergency vehicles parked out front her home. He said he was on his way over and that I should head home. I immediately called our next door neighbour to learn more and found out that my Mom was not in danger. Rather, it was our dear friend, Kerry.

Once home, I found the Minister and Mom seated in the living room talking about the wedding. I was unable to participate in the conversation because the phone rang and it was Revenue Canada. They had randomly selected me for a home visit and a friendly review of my books and business practices.

Tuesday, April 3, 2007

I was detained all day in Georgetown serving our client. The Irish Lad's only responsibility was to get to the bank. He did not. He was supposed to manage the wedding deposits. He did not.

Earlier this evening he had the gall to ask me for $1,200.00.

I declined.

He re-phrased the request to include a guaranteed return payment on Thursday. He knew for sure he could make it to the bank on Thursday. He even booked off the afternoon to attend to all wedding, real estate, automotive banking related matters.

I said no.

It's amazing how short a date can be when you don't hand over $1,200.

I had assisted him in the past and in turn he was always treating me to wonderful meals in restaurants and giving me small gifts. On one occasion, he gave me a copy of Scott's Directory software valued at many thousands of dollars for my small business. He heard about the hours that I was spending at the local library manually extracting and hand recording possible business leads.
I knew this time was different. His inability to make it to the bank was awash in red flags. Assisting him would result in my loss of much-needed money. Where the hell was the money from his trust fund or

Perfect Prey

employment? Clearly he had money to pay the rent, operate a car, eat extraordinarily well, dock a sail boat, pay for medical school and housing. He could manage an income property in London, England, but not come up with $1,200 for a highly anticipated car delivery?

Are all wealthy people that scatter brained?

Wednesday, April 4, 2007

I arrived home from work around 4:30 P.M. There he sat, on Mom's loveseat, huffing and puffing, visibly upset. I had noted that on my approach, I hadn't noticed his car.

The story was that his Ford Escape broke down on the highway near Markham Road and had to be towed to a local dealership. He made his way to Mom's in the hope that I would be here and eventually drive him home. He was not overly concerned about the repairs as he was anticipating the arrival of an Audi A6 at any time. This announcement allowed him to clarify his earlier request for the loan of $1,200.

The $1,200.00 was "just in case" the car was delivered before he made it to the bank Thursday afternoon. The car was from his Father's dealership in Montreal, the money was the fee for the driving service.

I remained firm and said no.

The Ford would be repaired and returned to a dealership as a used vehicle.

In full force, he continued to rant about the ambush attack of several police officers who pounded on his side door around 7:00 A.M. Without search warrants they made their way through his home allegedly in search of stolen goods reported by neighbours who were recently burglarized.

I immediately queried him about the warrant issued, stating that they could not enter without one. He agreed and quickly said that he would contact his new lawyer immediately about such conduct.

On the ride to his house, I asked him how he planned to go to work on Thursday much less get the banking done. He said that he would perform sales calls from home and his associate would make the in-person visits and that he'd take the bus to the bank.

Thursday, April 5, 2007

I worked for Suncor Energy Products until 2:00 P.M. I also had a ton of personal errands associated with Easter weekend and the arrival of my Brother and family on Good Friday. My cell rang while at work and it was the Irish Lad, out of breath. There had been a change of plans. His business associate, Dominic, picked him up to assist with the day's sales calls. Dominic would also drive him to the bank at Yonge and Sheppard around 1:30 P.M.

Working less than one mile down the road, I suggested he complete his banking and I would pick him up and together we would make rounds with our deposits. He said: "Great."

Perfect Prey

At 1:30 P.M. he called to say that he had been to the bank and was heading to his home. He asked me if I would pick him up there and give him a lift to Maple, Ontario, for a last minute sales appointment scheduled for 3 P.M. He knew this was over the top but needed my help. From there we would complete our wedding related errands.

I agreed.

I called him to let him know that I was five minutes away and he said he'd meet me outside on the sidewalk at the corner, a good block away from his home. Picture a 270 pound man wearing a heavy down filled ski jacket and a fur hat with ear covers on a spring day. Now ask yourself: Does that seem a little unusual?

We grinded our way up Highway 400 to Maple. Seconds away from the Major Mackenzie Road exit, he blurted out that his earlier trip to his bank was incomplete: code for didn't actually make it to the bank and organize our finances for the wedding.

He did possess a so-called commission based cheque made out by his associate Dominic. The problem was that it was going to be held for five business days until it cleared. Alternatively, he could take the cheque to Dom's bank, in Maple, have it certified and then redeem it at his local BMO branch. I saw the certified cheque for $2,000.

Back in the car I concluded that we were now on a mad dash south to Yonge and Sheppard to cash this cheque and complete his botched attempt at personal banking.

The Irish Lad went on about how he hated banks, line-ups, and the idea of having to ask an institution to give you what is rightfully yours much less proving that it is yours.

Traffic was too heavy to pay much notice. I was on Highway 401, heading eastbound to Yonge Street, and reminded the Irish Lad that we were approaching the exit near his bank.

He refused to go. Under no circumstances would he entertain lining up in a bank late Thursday afternoon before a long weekend. I asked him about the other banking. He said it will have to wait until Tuesday.

I could have spit blood. I was gripping the steering wheel imagining that it was his throat. *The Irish Lad's luck was about to run out and he knew it.*

His solution was to divert my attention with too much information:

Drive him to a Money Mart where he could cash this cheque and forward 100 Euros to his daughter via Western Union. (Points for being a good Dad.)

Return to the minivan and start talking about a big surprise waiting for me.

Ask me what I am doing on Tuesday between 10:00 A.M. and noon.

Ask me to call my insurance company and let them know that I would no longer need insurance for the minivan from Tuesday, April 10th.

Seek rate for a fully loaded Land Rover with a V8 engine, in hunter green with tan leather interior.

Seal the deal by suggesting dinner out somewhere special.

The Irish Lad went on about how he hated banks, line-ups, and the idea of having to ask an institution to give you what is rightfully yours much less proving that it is yours.

Traffic was too heavy to pay much notice. I was on Highway 401, heading eastbound to Yonge Street, and reminded the Irish Lad that we were approaching the exit near his bank.

He refused to go. Under no circumstances would he entertain lining up in a bank late Thursday afternoon before a long weekend. I asked him about the other banking. He said it will have to wait until Tuesday.

I could have spit blood. I was gripping the steering wheel imagining that it was his throat. *The Irish Lad's luck was about to run out and he knew it.*

His solution was to divert my attention with too much information:

Drive him to a Money Mart where he could cash this cheque and forward 100 Euros to his daughter via Western Union. (Points for being a good Dad.)

Return to the minivan and start talking about a big surprise waiting for me.

Ask me what I am doing on Tuesday between 10:00 A.M. and noon.

Ask me to call my insurance company and let them know that I would no longer need insurance for the minivan from Tuesday, April 10th.

Seek rate for a fully loaded Land Rover with a V8 engine, in hunter green with tan leather interior.

Seal the deal by suggesting dinner out somewhere special.

At 1:30 P.M. he called to say that he had been to the bank and was heading to his home. He asked me if I would pick him up there and give him a lift to Maple, Ontario, for a last minute sales appointment scheduled for 3 P.M. He knew this was over the top but needed my help. From there we would complete our wedding related errands.

I agreed.

I called him to let him know that I was five minutes away and he said he'd meet me outside on the sidewalk at the corner, a good block away from his home. Picture a 270 pound man wearing a heavy down filled ski jacket and a fur hat with ear covers on a spring day. Now ask yourself: Does that seem a little unusual?

We grinded our way up Highway 400 to Maple. Seconds away from the Major Mackenzie Road exit, he blurted out that his earlier trip to his bank was incomplete: code for didn't actually make it to the bank and organize our finances for the wedding.

He did possess a so-called commission based cheque made out by his associate Dominic. The problem was that it was going to be held for five business days until it cleared. Alternatively, he could take the cheque to Dom's bank, in Maple, have it certified and then redeem it at his local BMO branch. I saw the certified cheque for $2,000.

Back in the car I concluded that we were now on a mad dash south to Yonge and Sheppard to cash this cheque and complete his botched attempt at personal banking.

Remind me that he can't wait to meet my family on Good Friday.

Suggest I go home, catch my breath and meet with him for dinner in a couple of hours.

The Last Supper

The Irish Lad treated us to a wonderful seafood experience at a north Toronto restaurant called C-Food. He was in his happy place. With the chef at his side, the manager not far behind and the server catering to our every need, the Luck of the Irish had struck gold. He bought a round of drinks for the kitchen staff to be enjoyed at the end of their shift.

We strolled toward my minivan and he asked me to go for a nightcap at Safari, another wonderful spot on Avenue Road. We had a drink, while the Lad ordered a complete second dinner. It was if he was loading up in anticipation of going hungry. We did manage to communicate calmly. The storm had passed. A few pieces of shellfish, a modest wine and a kiss goodnight amounted to a successful mission for this military man. War was averted.

I drove the Irish Lad home. At his insistence, I was to drop him off at the corner, not in front of his house or on his driveway. The reason being I would not need to perform a u-turn and could head home for a good night's sleep. It was his intent to use the next day to clean and organize his home until it was time to meet and greet my family. It was his expectation to arrive at Mom's in an Audi A6.

Friday, April 6, 2007

I slept until 9:00 A.M. on Good Friday. The Irish Lad called, and Mom told him I was still asleep to which he responded that I should not be disturbed. At 10:35 A.M., I called him back. He started the conversation by telling me how much he loved and appreciated me. Mention of the cleaning frenzy, large deposits to the recycling bins, and laundry combined to create a welcoming environment as I was to be his weekend guest.

He anticipated the delivery of the Audi A6 in the late afternoon. It was his expectation to arrive at Mom's between 5:00 P.M. and 6:00 P.M.

Even though I had serious doubts about the Irish Lad's credibility, I was so thrilled to be able to host my Brother and family under such positive conditions. The past several years had not gone well for us as a group. There had been battles with cancer, relationship failures, personal and pet injuries, you name it. This time it would be different, indeed better.

Joanne, my sister-in-law, cornered me in the kitchen to test my commitment to this new man and the prospect of marriage. She asked me what happened to Mr. Date.Ca. Back in December, I was hiking up some God forsaken mudslide with Joanne. What kept me going was talk of Mr. Date.Ca and how I looked forward to getting this friendship off the ground. She was intrigued, and I kept her up to date with details. Then out of nowhere comes the Irish Lad. For both Matthew and Joanne, alarm bells were going off. They know me and my heart. They also know that I am running on empty.

Perfect Prey

I admitted that I had not ended it well, much less decidedly with Mr. Date.Ca.

I changed the subject to my divorce and how the law has not delivered a fair result for this beaten-up family.

It's 6:00 P.M. and I do not see an Audi A6 much less its driver. No answer on his cell or landline. I assumed he was on his way and didn't hear his phone ring because of the music pounding from the car's stereo system. We began eating appetizers, had a drink and talked about my future. I held back on several details about the wedding in favour of having us together to share our plans. Before we knew it, an hour had fled by and still no Audi A6 much less its driver. No answer on his cell or landline.

Not a great first impression for my Brother and family. Not a clue about what was going on with the Irish Lad. This was not normal at all. If anything, the Lad was always in our face, seldom arrived with advance warning and never missed an opportunity to meet new people for the purpose of holding court. I had to make an executive decision and serve dinner. It was 7:30 P.M.

Now there was an elephant on the dining room table blocking our view and conversation. Looks of: "I told you so" were forming on the faces of my visiting family. Mom gave it her best to remain hopeful, but at the 15 minute mark suggested that the Lad may have encountered some difficulty. She went on to remind me that he is an overweight middle-aged man who lives alone and who has been working physically hard all day.

I agreed to go to his home. I didn't offer to go. Behind the wheel, I continued to call his phones.

On arrival there was no sign of an Audi A6. At first, I knocked on the door, waited and then used my key. The stairwell lights were on as were the lights in the common living spaces including the laundry room. All that was left for me to do was unlock his apartment door. I did mutter the words, "please don't be dead."

I walked in, turned on the light and immediately noticed that Elvis had left the building.
The Lad's personal effects, including clothing, toiletries, preferred kitchen gadgets, and knives along with his laptop computer were all gone.

I did a quick sweep of the place and collected anything that belonged to me. I was able to move, breathe and think. I performed a second sweep of the apartment and noticed his cordless phone and new Dell printer.

Upstairs, I had noted the lights were on. The owners were celebrating Passover in Montreal. I ran upstairs to the main floor and was met by Carrie, the other house tenant.

Carrie looked terrified to see me and went as far as to take a step back even though she was behind a locked French door. I asked her where the Irish Lad had gone and though visibly shaken, she opened the door and invited me in. I would get the details later. Now I needed to call the police and my family. I suspected I had been conned by the Irish Lad, or was at least part of something worth addressing with the police.

Toronto Police suggested that this was not an emergency, nor had any crime been committed. They talked about how busy they were and that although they felt bad for me, they did not believe it to be a police matter.

I insisted that it was. I suggested that they run a check on the address of this house and connect the dots. I mentioned the presence of multiple officers described as entering the Lad's basement apartment and conducting an unlawful search for stolen goods. They agreed to send officers. I asked that they give me a couple of hours to return home and talk to my family before our discussion. I also wanted their visit to take place at Mom's house.

My next call was to Mom. I could only say the words, "He's gone." Her immediate reaction was to assume he had died. *I wish.* I repeated: "He's gone, left, I have been the victim of a con."

Mom demanded that I get the hell out of that house and come home. I told her I would as soon as I was able. I needed answers and wanted to talk to Carrie. I wanted to search his apartment for any clues that might explain the nature of his game.

Standing still in the kitchen, Carrie continued to stare at me until I broke the silence with a question. "What do you know about all of this? I asked. She said that the Irish Lad took her into his confidence and conveyed his concerns about my state of mind. He suggested that it was I that demanded we marry and his only recourse was to flee.

Carrie confirmed he left around 3:30 P.M. in an airport limo.

With that little information, I returned to the apartment and picked up his cordless phone. I began to view all missed or inbound calls. I even hit redial. I'll be damned, Airport Limo. The Lad left a pen and pad, very helpful indeed, so I made note of every last phone number stored.

It was my understanding that he even left a farewell note for the landlords, complete with the balance of his rent. I am assuming $1,200. You've got to respect a con artist, who thinks it's important to pay his rent. Granted, with other people's money, most of the time.

I returned to the upstairs living room and accepted Carrie's offer of a glass of water. She had relaxed enough to talk to me. Her description of the Irish Lad was one of being a creep. He made her feel uncomfortable and she couldn't put her finger on it.

I explained to her that I think there are many more layers to this onion than either of us had imagined. Then it occurred to me to ask her about the police raid on Wednesday.

Carrie's response confirmed my call to the police was not in vain. She said five officers came with a warrant and court order to tow away the Ford Escape. They did search his apartment and he was outraged. Later, the police assured Carrie that she was likely safe living in this house, but should keep the interior door locked at all times.

The Irish Lad told Carrie it was all a misunderstanding. The Ford belonged to both he and this woman, possibly his wife, from Ottawa. There was some confusion about whose turn it was to drive it. Kind of like whose turn it is to pay child support?

I suggested to Carrie that she call the owners and ask their permission to have the locks changed. She did, and the locksmith was on his way. The owners also called a close friend to spend the evening in the house as support for Carrie.

I felt dizzy and disgusted with myself. I wanted to jump into a vat of bleach and gargle with whiskey. I dreaded the drive home. I had been violated. I picked up my cell phone and called the Irish Lad. His voice mail kicked right in and I was very clear. I called him a monster and told him that I had reported him to the police. I ended the message with the warning that I would find him and God help him.

I called Louise, the Matron of Honour. She was completely horrified and wanted to come to my side. I told her I needed to attend to Tess and Rachel and would talk to her in the morning. I did ask her to cancel our bridal gown appointment for Saturday morning.

Hold your daughters and never let them go.

I arrived home around 10:00 P.M. and dealt with the important things first. I held my daughters in my arms and assured them of our safety. I explained that I was as confused as they were. We had not been the victims of a financial scam, nor had we lost our home.

We had our health and one another. The most important thing I said was that I alone would move us forward as a family. I would never allow anyone to sidetrack us again.

Then, under my breath, I vowed to track this son of a bitch down. I vowed to unleash a world of pain on his sorry ass; the kind of pain that would shed so much light on his fraudulent ways that he'd need a proctologist to remove the Blarney Stone.

I explained all that I knew to my Mom, Brother and Sister-in-Law. Then I went to the computer to check my e-mails. The Irish Lad had the gall to e-mail me using the lie that his Father had passed away and he had to travel to Dublin. This message arrived at 3:18 P.M. on Good Friday claiming to be from Logan Airport, in Boston. He must be a time traveler as he was observed leaving his home in Toronto at 3:30 P.M.

He also said he'd be in touch and loved me. Wait until he hears my voice mail!

I'm no expert, but I think my suggestion that GOD help him constitutes a break- up.

Part 3

Saturday, April 7, 2007

The Toronto Police arrived around 1:00 A.M. A male and female officer entered Mom's house with a prepared speech. The male officer wanted the facts while the female, with slightly tilted head and sympathetic tone, spoke about how painful it can be when someone you love gets cold feet.

They praised my logical attempt to try to piece together a reasonable explanation for his departure refusing to accept my suggestion that he is a con artist. They also assured me that the mental health steps I had taken are consistent with suggested effective coping methods (then they put away their training manual).

I could hear myself screaming bloody murder inside my head. With the little patience I had left, I asked them to run a check on their computer. They declined as it violated the Irish Lad's right to privacy. This was not acceptable and I kept at them. I described how we met on www.date.ca and the pace at which the relationship progressed. I described the wedding details and still they nodded sympathetically. Then I shifted gears. I told them I had seen his driver's licence and it confirmed his name, birth date, and most recent address in Ottawa. I also gave them his phone numbers. Still, they would not budge.

They were more concerned with how it was possible I was able to observe the private details of his driver's license. Their ignorance was astounding.

Then it hit me.

These officers had not done their due diligence. They had not run a background check based on my reporting call citing the Maplewood address. I wanted to cry. I blurted out that 48 hours prior, several police officers with a search warrant and a court order to tow his vehicle were at his home.

They agreed to go back to their car and run a check. Within five minutes they were back, heads lowered and slightly apologetic. They affirmed that he is known to police and was from Montreal, not Ireland. They finished by saying that I was to forget I ever met this man and get on with my life. Then they left. Unless they planned on inducing a coma, forgetting was not an option. I would find justice my own way.

I had to unravel the mess created by the Irish Lad. To do this, I first had to make a list for moving forward:

1. Protect my children and Mother from anyone that dares cross my path.
2. Cancel a wedding.
3. Communicate possible identity theft to bank and credit card companies.
4. Reach out to Mr. Date.Ca if only to let him know that I am an ass.
5. Expose the Irish Lad to www.date.ca
6. Expose the Irish Lad to car dealerships and real estate agencies.

Perfect Prey

7. Expose the Irish Lad to his present and past employers.

8. Find the son of a bitch and nail him.

9. Become a grown-up.

10, Pay off debt.

11. Create a life for my children and I that does not require the involvement of anyone other than me!

12. Pray.

Writing lists helps me to process pain. If I had money, shopping would work too.

Using the phone and e-mail I began cancelling the Vaughan Estate, the photographer, the Minister, not to mention alert the realty agent, the Land Rover dealership, my lawyer, www.date.ca, and the Lad's current employer. I prayed that I would not be held financially accountable for the credit card deposit made in my name. All parties, save one were gracious and let me off the hook.

The marriage preparation course dinged me for the full amount of the course fee. I deserve that hit as a reminder of my stupidity. It did occur to me to take the course anyway. This way I would have proof moving forward that I was qualified to get married.

My dating profile could be updated to reflect that I come with pre-marriage certification as well as a spare, unused divorce. That's right, I almost forgot to mention that when the Ontario Court misplaced my divorce, they countered by granting an extra one.

I did not perform these tasks alone as Tess, Rachel, nephew Dylan and niece Sidney remained glued to my side. Four children, indeed young adults had been introduced to the darker side of life in a very brief period of time. I prayed that this experience would serve as a teachable moment rather than a fascination.

The Irish Lad's landlord called from Montreal. I blindsided her as well. She had spoken with Carrie and knew about the locks being changed. I asked her how the con artist had come into their lives. She answered that he responded to an advertisement and sensing he needed a break, they gave him a chance. It was if he was starting again, rebuilding his life. He also came across as Jewish, speaking Yiddish and making every attempt to fit in. Rent was always on time and paid in cash. She had not run any kind of reference or background check.

I shared the Lad's version of how he came to live in her home and she was astounded. My references to his Irish accent and background were completely out of sync with the man they knew.

It's funny how things stick with you, like tumours, bad breath, and warts.

I remembered the Irish Lad's car came from Donnelly Ford Lincoln Motors in Ottawa. My brother, Matthew, works in Ottawa and I gave him this information. The day had gotten away from me. It was time to seek refuge in my bed.

It was time to e-mail Mr. Date.Ca. I did and he responded.

He suggested that I meet him at his office on Easter Monday and we head out for lunch. I agreed, signed off and began praying.

introduced to the darker side of life in a very brief period of time. I prayed that this experience would serve as a teachable moment rather than a fascination.

The Irish Lad's landlord called from Montreal. I blindsided her as well. She had spoken with Carrie and knew about the locks being changed. I asked her how the con artist had come into their lives. She answered that he responded to an advertisement and sensing he needed a break, they gave him a chance. It was if he was starting again, rebuilding his life. He also came across as Jewish, speaking Yiddish and making every attempt to fit in. Rent was always on time and paid in cash. She had not run any kind of reference or background check.

I shared the Lad's version of how he came to live in her home and she was astounded. My references to his Irish accent and background were completely out of sync with the man they knew.

It's funny how things stick with you, like tumours, bad breath, and warts.

I remembered the Irish Lad's car came from Donnelly Ford Lincoln Motors in Ottawa. My brother, Matthew, works in Ottawa and I gave him this information. The day had gotten away from me. It was time to seek refuge in my bed.

It was time to e-mail Mr. Date.Ca. I did and he responded.

He suggested that I meet him at his office on Easter Monday and we head out for lunch. I agreed, signed off and began praying.

7. Expose the Irish Lad to his present and past employers.
8. Find the son of a bitch and nail him.
9. Become a grown-up.
10, Pay off debt.
11. Create a life for my children and I that does not require the involvement of anyone other than me!
12. Pray.

Writing lists helps me to process pain. If I had money, shopping would work too.

Using the phone and e-mail I began cancelling the Vaughan Estate, the photographer, the Minister, not to mention alert the realty agent, the Land Rover dealership, my lawyer, www.date.ca, and the Lad's current employer. I prayed that I would not be held financially accountable for the credit card deposit made in my name. All parties, save one were gracious and let me off the hook.

The marriage preparation course dinged me for the full amount of the course fee. I deserve that hit as a reminder of my stupidity. It did occur to me to take the course anyway. This way I would have proof moving forward that I was qualified to get married.

My dating profile could be updated to reflect that I come with pre-marriage certification as well as a spare, unused divorce. That's right, I almost forgot to mention that when the Ontario Court misplaced my divorce, they countered by granting an extra one.

I did not perform these tasks alone as Tess, Rachel, nephew Dylan and niece Sidney remained glued to my side. Four children, indeed young adults had been

Perfect Prey

Sunday, April 8, 2007

Easter dinner was peaceful and strangely normal. This does not mean that we moved on unscathed. Rather, the air seemed fresher. The sudden end of this charade resulted in a much-needed calm for our household. I allowed my family to believe that calmer days were ahead. That was the least that I could do. I had no intention of sitting still until the capture of this predator. Christ may have died for out sins, but I wanted to take this particular bastard down alive. I figured that Christ had a long enough list to take responsibility for.

Empathy, not pity came our way. Tess believed that the Irish Lad was going to replace all that was lost by the abandonment of her Father. Why wouldn't she believe him? He met her with arms open wide and expressed respect for her intelligence and spoke of loving her as one of his own. Let's face it, what child doesn't want two parents surrounded by a mansion, yacht, international travel, and a cool car?

Rachel remained focused on my face as if looking for any sign that I was about to snap. She held on for dear life unaware that I had snapped well before I ever met the Irish Lad.

Mom, as always, had my back.

I draw strength from these women and vowed to make good decisions, take necessary risks and make them proud. I am taking back my life, and I will leverage every aspect of my personal strength to emerge whole. The hunted will become the hunter.

Nothing would ever be the same in my life. The consequences of my actions converged in a bottleneck bursting to be set free. My days as a doormat were over. I fashioned myself as a moving sidewalk. I would not rest until everything in my life had been improved, at my own hand.

Mom, Matt and Jo all begged me to step off and let the police handle this fiasco. But the police had not listened. The Lad was not a person of concern at this time. I was on my own. They did not realize that the harm had been done, and now it was my turn to force the hand of justice. I know this scumbag is not worth the effort, but my sanity is.

Don't ask yourself what the world needs; ask yourself what makes you come alive. And then go do that. Because what the world needs are people who have come alive.
    - Harold Whitman

Perfect Prey

Monday, April 9, 2007

Everything has changed

Matt, Jo and the children made their way back to Quebec. Holding my Brother close, I reminded him to check out the dealership in Ottawa. I am the Hunter.

I made my way for the shower knowing that I had one opportunity to face off with Mr. Date.Ca. I dared not expect anything. I deserved less than nothing. I went to apologize. Part of me resisted the apology part as I felt he owed me a few of his own for falsely representing himself as divorced.

Seated in his office, I began my defence. I said that I was an idiot who had placed a price on my heart in an effort to wipe out the debt created by my ex-Husband. The con artist sold me a quick fix, and I was desperate. And though the con artist did manage to sweep me off my feet from time to time, he never had my heart.

The lessons learned were that I alone had to face my responsibilities moving forward. Rebuilding my life and that of my children's lives most certainly fell within my abilities.

I dared not speak of love.

Mr. Date.Ca held me for the longest time. We kissed. Then he returned to the other side of his desk and continued to work. I felt like I was in the principal's office waiting for the secretary to come in and suggest I leave. So I began to gesture that I was in fact leaving.

He returned to the table, yet kept his distance. I waited. The pain in his face and in the tone of his voice was heart wrenching. I remained attentive and silent, allowing him to give me my lumps and say his piece. I apologized again and affirmed that I expected nothing from him. My visit was to assure him that he is a wonderful and worthy man.

I had dropped the ball again. I had stepped back into my doormat role. I needed to clarify his marital status and shrunk under the pressure of the moment. Bullshit, nothing had changed; I am still at the mercy of men.

The tension was agonizing.

He stood up and said, "Let's go, I'm hungry." I couldn't believe it.

Standing toe to toe we resumed our embrace and kissed. I decided to test my luck by suggesting that we see each other on Friday, April 13th for dinner. He accepted. This meant that I was going to miss my marriage preparation course and possibly save my own soul.

Paging Dr. Siobhan Hill?

I began to think about my e-mail communication with his so-called daughter, Siobhan, and quickly realized that I was in fact communicating with the Irish Lad. The question was: Who was this young woman portrayed in the photograph? The Irish Lad is a dangerous man. I needed to find out just how dangerous.

Tuesday, April 10, 2007

Matt paid the dealership a visit and learned the Irish Lad, was the Scottish Lad while working as a salesperson from June to August 2006 for Donnelly Ford. They referred to him as a con man. They also confirmed that he was driving a customer's car. The game was afoot.

I reported the Irish Lad to his current employer, the Ontario Energy Savings Corporation, and the general manager took it lightly. They would consider the possibility of conducting an informal review. Stunned by his lack of concern, I asked how it was possible for a company who holds the public trust selling utilities to hire such a person.

Did they perform their due diligence by running his driver's licence? Did they check or even ask for references? In response, they told me that running such checks were not required for commissioned-based employees.

The Lad managed to dodge rather ordinary reference check processes. Donnelly Ford did not run a check. Ontario Energy Savings Corporation did not run a check, nor did his previous employer, Universal Energy Corporation.

What the hell is going on?

I decided to dig a little deeper and review the list of telephone numbers I had recorded from the Lad's phone. Many of the numbers were familiar such as my own, his workplace, etc. Then I saw one that identified his co-worker, Dom.

I called the number and Dom's wife answered. A sweet and helpful person, thank God, I began to set the stage for my call. Once I had her confidence that I was on the up and up, I encouraged her to contact her Husband immediately if only to protect him from the risk of financial loss. I mentioned that we were at his bank on the previous Thursday to get a personal cheque of Dom's certified.

I shared every conceivable piece of contact information about how I could be reached with her in the hopes that Dom would make contact. He did not. I believe he was under a gag order by his employer. I also suspect that the Lad had taken Dom for several thousand dollars and the embarrassment outweighed his better judgment.

Donnelly Ford Lincoln Motors

I telephoned the car dealership's 1-800 number and asked to speak with the Human Resources Manager. Fay, a seasoned professional, responded to my call and offered useful information. Careful to protect the business, the customers, and her integrity as an H.R. professional, I had found a connection to the Irish Lad's recent past.

I had to ask Fay how it was possible that they would even hire such a fraud. Her only defence was the truth. She was out of town on holiday when he was hired. On her return, she immediately sensed something wasn't quite right, but that was insufficient to warrant his dismissal. The leasing manager also signed off on the Lad's co-lease of the Ford Escape without running a credit check on him.

I called the number and Dom's wife answered. A sweet and helpful person, thank God, I began to set the stage for my call. Once I had her confidence that I was on the up and up, I encouraged her to contact her Husband immediately if only to protect him from the risk of financial loss. I mentioned that we were at his bank on the previous Thursday to get a personal cheque of Dom's certified.

I shared every conceivable piece of contact information about how I could be reached with her in the hopes that Dom would make contact. He did not. I believe he was under a gag order by his employer. I also suspect that the Lad had taken Dom for several thousand dollars and the embarrassment outweighed his better judgment.

Donnelly Ford Lincoln Motors

I telephoned the car dealership's 1-800 number and asked to speak with the Human Resources Manager. Fay, a seasoned professional, responded to my call and offered useful information. Careful to protect the business, the customers, and her integrity as an H.R. professional, I had found a connection to the Irish Lad's recent past.

I had to ask Fay how it was possible that they would even hire such a fraud. Her only defence was the truth. She was out of town on holiday when he was hired. On her return, she immediately sensed something wasn't quite right, but that was insufficient to warrant his dismissal. The leasing manager also signed off on the Lad's co-lease of the Ford Escape without running a credit check on him.

Tuesday, April 10, 2007

Matt paid the dealership a visit and learned the Irish Lad, was the Scottish Lad while working as a salesperson from June to August 2006 for Donnelly Ford. They referred to him as a con man. They also confirmed that he was driving a customer's car. The game was afoot.

I reported the Irish Lad to his current employer, the Ontario Energy Savings Corporation, and the general manager took it lightly. They would consider the possibility of conducting an informal review. Stunned by his lack of concern, I asked how it was possible for a company who holds the public trust selling utilities to hire such a person.

Did they perform their due diligence by running his driver's licence? Did they check or even ask for references? In response, they told me that running such checks were not required for commissioned-based employees.

The Lad managed to dodge rather ordinary reference check processes. Donnelly Ford did not run a check. Ontario Energy Savings Corporation did not run a check, nor did his previous employer, Universal Energy Corporation.

What the hell is going on?

I decided to dig a little deeper and review the list of telephone numbers I had recorded from the Lad's phone. Many of the numbers were familiar such as my own, his workplace, etc. Then I saw one that identified his co-worker, Dom.

I wanted to reach the customer whose car was borrowed by the Irish Lad. I need to know if she had pressed charges, or at least reported it to the dealership. She had.

Fay was able to provide me with a contact number for the victim's lawyer. I thanked her and promised to keep her in the loop.

Wednesday, April 11, 2007

Mom was attending a follow-up appointment at the Orthopedic and Arthritic Hospital. I figured that I would take a walk and make the call on my cell to this lawyer. He was cooperative, and equally frustrated by his client's battle with the Irish Lad. I asked him to tell his client about me and give her the choice to contact me.

I no sooner walked through Mom's front door and my phone rang. It was Darlene, the Ottawa victim. One became two. There is truth to the saying that there is strength in numbers.

The details of Darlene's personal involvement are not important, as the pattern remains consistent with respect to how the Lad spins his romantic scam. Look to my own experience if you need reminding.

One significant difference is that while I was 44, Darlene was in her early 60s. Age is irrelevant to a con artist.

Perfect Prey

Darlene's Story (as told in her own words.):

I met him at Daniel O'Connell's Pub in March 2006, where he worked as a cook. I had a conversation with him. I told him that my Husband was in a Long Term Care facility. This was his cue! He gave me a hug and told me he helped his Aunt with her Husband who had Alzheimer's disease. What a croc! How stupid I was! Anyway, things went south from there.

We leased the Ford Escape in June 2006 from Donnelly Ford, South Bank! My lawyer, Matt Gervan said it was an elaborate scheme, a con. He (the Lad) worked at Donnelly at the time. They did not check his credit rating for the lease or his background when they hired him. The HR person was really upset when she found out they had hired him.

The reason we/he got the lease was because of the money my Husband and I brought into the dealership. Well, basically me.

He stole the vehicle in October when he left on the 18th. He told me in an e-mail he would pay the lease. Of course, he didn't. I stopped the payments. Ford Credit called me in January. My lawyer had spoken to them to get them to look for the vehicle. I had hired a private investigator to look for it. I got the address on Maplewood Avenue from Rogers who had been calling me looking for the slob.

The first investigator said that they had gone to the address and he wasn't there. In the meantime, Dave Laroche, Ford Credit, had been calling me and I asked him why Ford Credit hadn't told the police that the vehicle had been stolen. It was stolen, but he said it wasn't because his name was on the lease as a primary. He wasn't paying for the truck, had taken it and disappeared with it, but they wouldn't say it had been stolen or have the police look for it.

In January when he called me, he told me if I didn't start paying for the SUV and the arrears he would send my name to the Credit Bureau. Basically, what he did was blackmail me to start paying for the bloody truck. I paid the arrears for November and December and have been paying ever since. They won't take his name off the lease because he is a primary.

My lawyer was going to try and get a court order to have his name taken off. He wasn't sure if he would be successful. He said if he got the same judge who gave the court order to retrieve the vehicle in April 2007, it wouldn't be a problem. He wasn't sure if he would get him. That would have been more money – $2,000-$3,000 – spent. I'd already spent a considerable amount of money.

Anyway, I spoke to Julian at Ford Credit in June. I said I was going to take the vehicle back to Donnelly Ford. He said if I did that he would give my name to the Credit Bureau.

They know he is a criminal, a con man. It doesn't matter. I'm paying for the bloody truck, and they still won't remove his name. If they did get a court order, they would need his address to sign it.

I didn't want my name given to the Credit Bureau. I called Visa and they said I'd still be able to use my credit card, but they would not be able to increase my limit.

Anyway, Donnelly Ford did not check his background when they hired him. They did not run a credit check when he signed the lease. Had they done so, they would have seen that he had been in jail or was at least seeing a parole officer.

At this point I wanted to vomit. I had been active as a passenger in Darlene's car from late January until April. Then it hit me, the private investigator looking for the Lad had likely been watching us, waiting to apprehend the vehicle.

There was nothing I could do to change that fact. Still, I wanted to help Darlene with her struggle at Ford Credit.

I asked Darlene to describe the Lad's behaviour, anything that would lead me toward more information resulting in his capture. She had noted his use of an anti-psychotic medication typically prescribed to manage hallucinations and bi-polar disorder.

She had also noted his fervent search for old "classmates" on the Internet.

I called Fay at Donnelly and lobbied on Darlene's behalf. Although sympathetic, Fay had her hands tied as the vehicle was property of Ford Leasing, a separate company.

Frustrated for Darlene, I knew that I needed to build a case to support her claim. This sounds crazy. I am not a police detective – it's just that the Ottawa Fraud Investigation Unit discarded her claim of being defrauded just as the Toronto Police discarded my own concerns.

Once again I found myself making lists. It occurred to me that maybe I knew more about the Irish Lad than I realized and before long, I came up with three pages, ordered alphabetically, all referencing his social connections, employers, family, hobbies, former residences, you name it. It was at this precise moment that I had crossed the point of no return. I was on the case.

Access to various search engines such as Google made it relatively easy to confirm the accuracy of certain references. The challenge was how to gain background information about a man with an extremely common name, John Hill.

As if by divine intervention I was inspired to go a different route. Using Google, I entered the Irish Lad's hotmail user identification: Bigfellow6633.

Split seconds later, there he was in an MSN chatroom called Verdun Connections. I followed his stream of communication and it seemed he was looking for his long-lost Mom. He had made significant references to his father, a local Verdun, Quebec, mechanic, and to his maternal Grandparents.

My reaction was swift. Contact the site manager and report the S.O.B. I did not want him removed, I just wanted them on alert and to inform them of my ordeal and my need to keep tabs. My allegations were not taken seriously.

Thursday, April 12, 2007

I shared this small breakthrough with Darlene. I wanted her to know that I was making progress, and she in turn confirmed the Lad was always on-line searching for his next female wallet. She also alluded to possible criminal activity and time served based on the findings of her private investigation.

I have momentum. I also have many other demands including single motherhood, wellness consultant, daughter, and family court punching bag.

Early May 2007

I recalled my intention to Google the Fish Café, located in Kerrisdale, B.C. and make contact with its owner.

Successful on the first attempt, I managed to speak with the owner who spared a few seconds recalling the Irish Lad but only as a petty thief and busboy/kitchen helper.

I was able to leave my contact information and was told that I could expect to hear from another victim, Marty Lemish.

That name was so familiar. By God, the Lad referenced him as a former business associate in the Rag

Trade from Montreal when he was chatting with Isaac, the Land Rover salesman.

While waiting to hear from Marty, I decided to pursue the Lad's restaurant work history. As employers go, it is easy to work under the table in various capacities in restaurants, all the while taking advantage of customers and making contacts. Simple slights of hand cost many customers their cell phones while in the Lad's presence.

Darlene was instrumental in this pursuit. She provided the names of a number of restaurants, all of which had direct dealings with the Irish Lad in Ottawa. He had always claimed that he either co-owned or helped to "reorganize," them. To the latter point, the Lad took credit for the reorganization of Fils Diner owned by West Park Lanes Ltd.

When I contacted them their response, and I quote was: *"Liz, time is limited and that man is really not worth any of ours. He worked here for a few months; he was a pretty good cook but reorganize my business??!!!! Please, **not** that person. He never conned anyone related directly to me so I am not sure exactly how he works. The police were here to see me as well and I am afraid I cannot offer any help. Any contact I had was probably useless from the moment he gave it to me. Sorry, I hope everything works out for you."*
  - **Rick.**

The other employer referred to him as a vile creature lacking in the talent needed to do anything of significance in any restaurant.

Perfect Prey

Marty Lemish's Story:

Much like Darlene, Marty wasted no time making his identity known to me. Marty's story was bound to be different as it did not involve romance. His con still falls under the definition of confidence scams resulting in the loss of money, goods and time. From the first moment I spoke with Marty, I determined him to be a Good Samaritan whose values gave way to unleashing a monster. Who was I kidding? the Irish Lad is and always will be a monster.

Marty made contact by telephone and e-mail. His rage had been quarantined since 2005. Hearing each other's story liberated Marty from quarantine, along with his considerable rage. Now we were three.

Marty's story needs to be told. It affirms that gender, personal economics, education, and stage of life do not assure one's immunity from fraud. I will speak to these important points of fact in the final section of the book. But now, back to Marty:

Recently widowed and preparing for a residential move, Marty decided to offer the heavy lifting work to men who were down on their luck. An active member of the Jewish community, Marty called on the Jewish Community Services organization to enlist the help of able-bodied men. In doing so he could provide them with work and compensation. The Irish Lad was one of the residents.

Homeless and shoeless, he presented as being able. There must have been something redeemable, even likeable about the Irish Lad because Marty continued to find him odd jobs and even aided him with new clothing. Sadly, he also invited him into his personal life, making it possible for the Lad to gain access to Marty's computer and sensitive files. Marty introduced the Lad to the owner of the Fish Café, setting the scene for the Lad to broaden his circle of influence and harm.

Frequent communication with Marty enabled me to learn many more horrible facts about the Irish Lad. I had access to police reports and now an article that clearly stated his conviction back in 1992 in Vancouver. The Lad posed as Hill and Associates, a computer consulting company. He managed to secure the confidence of the chief financial officer from the University of British Columbia. He also managed to forge the CFO's signature on a purchase order for $220,000 worth of computer equipment. This was beginning to look like the tip of the iceberg.

Marty went on to link the Lad's underhanded dealings with two other women. One is the victim of romantic fraud from Alberta and the other a victim of theft in Montreal. The latter victim had him dead to rights. He had defrauded the tenants of her apartment building, pretending to be the superintendent, collecting rent cheques. Computer equipment also went missing from several units. The details are a little fuzzy, but the sense is that he got away in the nick of time. I believe this may have been the crime that financed his road trip to Ottawa and Darlene. I do not know for certain.

Too much information going nowhere, and I needed to find someone in the media to help me to give life to my facts. My first thought was to forward a synopsis of my storyline to Canadian Living Magazine's Editor-in-Chief because of our mutual connection to the Irish Lad.

I do not think of myself as someone who "knows people." I think of myself as someone who helps people. I went back on Google and searched stories about con artists in Canada, and made note of an article written by investigative reporter Joe Warmington from the Toronto Sun.

I e-mailed Mr. Warmington about my experience and he replied. He was intrigued, but not convinced that the print media was the place for this story. The Sun would be an ideal vehicle to report the entire story once the con was captured.

Hearing this information did not discourage me from moving forward. I mentioned my effort to attract the Toronto Sun to Louise, my recently fired Matron of Honour. Louise reminded me that her brother Mike was on crew with CTV's investigative journalism program W-Five. As luck would have it, I ran into the local Dominion Food Store for groceries on the way home and, by God, ran into her brother, Mike. He had been briefed by Louise and was eager to assist. He handed me a business card suggesting I e-mail him the story AS SOON AS POSSIBLE. I don't even remember driving home.

For the first time in years, I was in the right place at the right time.

My family impressed by my tenacity, increasingly feared for my safety. They believe I am crazed with the notion of revenge. I am not crazed, I am inspired. Victims of the Irish Lad will have a voice.

Mr. Date.Ca is not thrilled by my plan to hunt down the Irish Lad. He wants me to leave it alone and move forward. This does not mean with him, beside him or on

Perfect Prey

record as his girlfriend. I am among his priorities, but remain unofficial.

I am not that woman. I will do no such thing. I am everything to my daughters. I have brought harm their way and now I must remove that threat.

I dance between being a victim of romantic fraud and divorce. Divorce has taught me there is no justice; fraud has taught me the same. Divorce has also taught me to separate the emotion from the business of getting to the bottom line; fraud the same. Divorce becomes a crime when your children do not receive court ordered child support; fraud is a crime – period. Divorce pervades our Nation, as does fraud. Both attract a great deal of attention without real risk of enforcement.

Divorce and fraud leave a trail of broken pieces and bruised souls. I can't find peace while living in pieces.
Now middle-aged, divorced, penniless and a victim of fraud, I must super-glue our lives back together. I may never fully seal the fine lines and cracks and this scares the hell out of me.

Con artists fly under the radar of the law. I have begun to regard myself as the control tower. The Irish Lad's flight will most likely try to seek permission to land in someone else's wallet. I intend to see that he never lands anywhere decent people live. Marty often refers to the Lad as a cockroach. To catch a cockroach, you need to shine the light on it. My plan is to light up the runway and then set it on fire.

Staying in constant communication with the Irish Lad's victims gives me strength. I rally their enthusiasm by keeping them abreast of my progress.

To date I have made contact with W-Five as well as Canadian Living Magazine. I am confident that either form of media will commit. I assure them that I will do everything in my power to find the Irish Lad and shine the light on this sociopath's repugnant face.

June 2007

I heard from W-Five's Senior Field Producer, Robert. His track record for investigative journalism is exact. He has guts and inspires confidence. My timing is problematic. The show is about to go on hiatus. As I understand it, W-Five uses the spring and early summer to cast a wide net aimed at attracting possible storylines. I am invited to visit with Robert down at the Globe and Mail building on Front Street in Toronto.

This is quite possibly the most exciting appointment I have ever had short of attending a fertility clinic. Standing in front of this iconic building reminds me of how far I have come in such a short time. Closing the deal is paramount.

Robert is made aware of my arrival in the building. I remain seated clutching my binder containing files and notes about the Irish Lad and his victims. We meet, we have coffee and I hand over what appears to be the work of an obsessive-compulsive. He notes that my attention to detail probably served as a little therapy and acknowledges that my efforts are worth further consideration. The only outstanding business for Robert at this time is the whereabouts of the Irish Lad. He deems this my homework. I must find him.

To date I have made contact with W-Five as well as Canadian Living Magazine. I am confident that either form of media will commit. I assure them that I will do everything in my power to find the Irish Lad and shine the light on this sociopath's repugnant face.

June 2007

I heard from W-Five's Senior Field Producer, Robert. His track record for investigative journalism is exact. He has guts and inspires confidence. My timing is problematic. The show is about to go on hiatus. As I understand it, W-Five uses the spring and early summer to cast a wide net aimed at attracting possible storylines. I am invited to visit with Robert down at the Globe and Mail building on Front Street in Toronto.

This is quite possibly the most exciting appointment I have ever had short of attending a fertility clinic. Standing in front of this iconic building reminds me of how far I have come in such a short time. Closing the deal is paramount.

Robert is made aware of my arrival in the building. I remain seated clutching my binder containing files and notes about the Irish Lad and his victims. We meet, we have coffee and I hand over what appears to be the work of an obsessive-compulsive. He notes that my attention to detail probably served as a little therapy and acknowledges that my efforts are worth further consideration. The only outstanding business for Robert at this time is the whereabouts of the Irish Lad. He deems this my homework. I must find him.

Perfect Prey

record as his girlfriend. I am among his priorities, but remain unofficial.

I am not that woman. I will do no such thing. I am everything to my daughters. I have brought harm their way and now I must remove that threat.

I dance between being a victim of romantic fraud and divorce. Divorce has taught me there is no justice; fraud has taught me the same. Divorce has also taught me to separate the emotion from the business of getting to the bottom line; fraud the same. Divorce becomes a crime when your children do not receive court ordered child support; fraud is a crime – period. Divorce pervades our Nation, as does fraud. Both attract a great deal of attention without real risk of enforcement.

Divorce and fraud leave a trail of broken pieces and bruised souls. I can't find peace while living in pieces.
Now middle-aged, divorced, penniless and a victim of fraud, I must super-glue our lives back together. I may never fully seal the fine lines and cracks and this scares the hell out of me.

Con artists fly under the radar of the law. I have begun to regard myself as the control tower. The Irish Lad's flight will most likely try to seek permission to land in someone else's wallet. I intend to see that he never lands anywhere decent people live. Marty often refers to the Lad as a cockroach. To catch a cockroach, you need to shine the light on it. My plan is to light up the runway and then set it on fire.

Staying in constant communication with the Irish Lad's victims gives me strength. I rally their enthusiasm by keeping them abreast of my progress.

Insanely overconfident, I agree and promise to find him. I am Nancy Drew.

My instincts, more useful now that I am available to pay attention to them, take me back to Calgary. This city makes sense to me. It is large enough, booming and to my knowledge does not play host to outstanding warrants for the Lad's arrest. I began to source other online dating sites. Then I remembered the lovely Siobhan's e-mail address; www.campus.ie which is Ireland's equivalent to Hotmail.

Once on the site, I enter the Internet arm, which is www.online.ie. I click on employment and note that it is a bulletin board. Quickly scanning down the first page I suddenly spot 'cobhman,' one of the Lad's user identifications. It reads Calgary, Alberta, Canada: Jobs on Offer. This means the Lad is searching for work in Calgary by re-routing the source of his inquiry through Ireland. The posting was April 17th. I pray I am not too late.

It turns out that this link connects to a dating site called Match.Com, and, I'll be damned, his membership information complete with picture supported by the current date has him named as John Hill, age 49, a member since 2/25/2007 (he was cheating on me), *and he's in Calgary.*

I can honestly say that Robert didn't anticipate hearing back from me within 24 hours.

Now we had a location. We needed to determine how to proceed. I suggested that we attract the Irish Lad using a false dating profile. I met him on www.date.ca, but had him banned back in April when I realized his game. There are only a few significant sites to work from, all permitting limited browsing without membership. If you want more than this limited browsing you are required to enlist with credit card in hand.

Back on my computer, I went to the other major site, Lavalife.com. I entered a few key descriptors about the Lad and went as far as to guess his user I.D. This time I tried the Irish Lad rather than Bigfellow6633. His profile fell from the sky onto my screen.

The plan was falling into place as was W-Five's hiatus along with my own two week vacation scheduled for the last two weeks of July. Robert assigned an associate producer to work with me in his absence.

For the next several weeks, I would rely on Robert's associate, Chad, to sustain my momentum. The plan called for me to enlist on Lavalife using my credit card for payment only while the profile would be fabricated by the crew at W-Five.

Early July 2007

With the help of a CTV producer's photographs, we created a profile that was so cheeky it was laughable. We went as far to give her the surname, Conroy. Her first name is Shelagh spelled in the traditional Irish way.

Within hours, The Lad had taken the bait. No doubt the crew was as amused as I by the speed at which we had him in our midst.

Perfect Prey

The Lad was flying for free on Lavalife. His limited capacity for communication was restricted to canned responses defined by Lavalife. Membership required a credit card, and I knew he did not possess one. This meant trouble. The Lad would have to suggest that Shelagh and he step out of their virtual world and pick up the phone.

As predicted, he provided his cell phone number and encouraged our lovely Shelagh to reach out and touch him. We were in trouble. W-Five is on break until August 20 and it is early July. The Irish Lad needs to land a meal ticket and we cannot follow through. Robert suggested that we lead the Lad to believe that Shelagh, though interested, is bound by previously scheduled vacation plans, but will call him on her return to arrange a coffee date.

Shelagh fired off the message and within moments is told by the Lad that he is seeking a woman whose priorities are in keeping with his own. Then he wished her well.

Robert instructs Chad to invite their associate from Calgary into the fold. A private investigator may be our only way to bridge the time gap in the days ahead. We have the Lad's cell phone number as a potential lead and suggest that the P.I. go on a pub crawl mindful of his physical description and with a photo of his face. It is Stampede season and the bars are packed.

While on holiday at Killbear Provincial Park, I made certain to check in with Chad. On one occasion there was a voice mail from Canadian Living. They had finally read my synopsis and wanted to interview me for the February 2008 edition. My concern was two-fold:

conflict with W-Five and being the magazine's Stupid Cupid for Valentine's Day readers. I called Chad and explained the situation. His response was clear in that I was able to be interviewed provided the television episode's air date preceded the magazines release date. The problem was he did not know what Robert had in mind regarding final production and release.

Then it hit me. I did it. I had attracted print and electronic media. The story of John Hill would be told. I was on Cloud Nine and feeling buried alive all at the same time.

August 2007

I met with Chad to discuss the next steps. We had not identified the whereabouts of the Lad in Calgary. We had no real idea if he was in Calgary. We did not know our status, nor the likelihood of risk of becoming that story that fell to the bottom of the pile awaiting completion. Chad would communicate with Robert and in turn give me my marching orders. It was August 14th, and we had to confirm the Lad's location.

We agreed to start where we left off. Shelagh Conroy had to send the Irish Lad a brief e-mail that simply stated "Back from vacation, making changes, interested in going for coffee?

Within a couple of minutes the Irish Lad took the bait and agreed to a first date. If this wasn't so serious a matter it would be comical.

I reminded the crew that he would want to talk on the phone. W-Five realized the need to have an active

Perfect Prey

cell phone shipped from Calgary for Shelagh to use. While waiting, we e-mailed the Lad back to request confirmation of his cell phone number and to let him know that it was going to be a busy week for Shelagh because she had to address family matters in Saskatoon. However, coffee was guaranteed if he would be patient and agree to Saturday, August 25th.

He was in agreement.

It was then it hit me. I was going to Calgary to face John Melvin Hill on camera for all friends, family and colleagues to see. All I could think about was placing my hands around his neck and pulling his throat out. All I could feel was fear and loathing,

Marty called me during the evening on Wednesday, August 22nd to tell me where the Lad worked. He had re-invented himself, this time as a so-called Kitchen Manager/Chef for a restaurant called Broken City. I was very appreciative and passed this information along to Robert.

Meanwhile, the Lad had called Shelagh Conroy to tell her that if she wanted a preview of what to expect from him, she was to tune into Calgary's Breakfast Television on Friday morning.

This was unbelievable. Seldom does the person of interest to a program like W-Five confirm his whereabouts and confirm an aspect of his fraudulent ways on television, hours before the arrival of the W-Five crew.

He was a "chef." This was hysterical. He has managed to gain employment without credentials and avoided another reference check. He has connected this well-meaning establishment with the media effectively promoting they will hire just about anyone to prepare food.

In the face of all of this chaos, I managed to hold the interest and affection of Mr. Date.Ca. Why on earth I am trying so hard speaks to my feelings of emptiness. I know that he is troubled by my decision to hunt the Irish Lad as am I. I try to keep him on point by reminding him how important it is for me to meet anyone from his family or social circle.

It frustrates Mr. Date.Ca when I refer to my role with men as a doormat, but that is exactly what I allowed in both my marriage and in my relationship with the Irish Lad. It will be through my actions and the result of those actions that I am able to destroy this damaging self-image. *Wanna bet? It's never that easy.*

My children are at the root of this need. I failed to act decisively when their Father left our marriage. The adage "he who hesitates is lost" nails my experience. I acted out of love, which meant trust. I trusted that this man who I loved and honoured would never dishonour his commitment to our children.

With the Irish Lad, I acted out of fear. I failed to trust in myself and made myself and my family a target for manipulation.

The gloves are off.

avoided another reference check. He has connected this well-meaning establishment with the media effectively promoting they will hire just about anyone to prepare food.

In the face of all of this chaos, I managed to hold the interest and affection of Mr. Date.Ca. Why on earth I am trying so hard speaks to my feelings of emptiness. I know that he is troubled by my decision to hunt the Irish Lad as am I. I try to keep him on point by reminding him how important it is for me to meet anyone from his family or social circle.

It frustrates Mr. Date.Ca when I refer to my role with men as a doormat, but that is exactly what I allowed in both my marriage and in my relationship with the Irish Lad. It will be through my actions and the result of those actions that I am able to destroy this damaging self-image. *Wanna bet? It's never that easy.*

My children are at the root of this need. I failed to act decisively when their Father left our marriage. The adage "he who hesitates is lost" nails my experience. I acted out of love, which meant trust. I trusted that this man who I loved and honoured would never dishonour his commitment to our children.

With the Irish Lad, I acted out of fear. I failed to trust in myself and made myself and my family a target for manipulation.

The gloves are off.

cell phone shipped from Calgary for Shelagh to use. While waiting, we e-mailed the Lad back to request confirmation of his cell phone number and to let him know that it was going to be a busy week for Shelagh because she had to address family matters in Saskatoon. However, coffee was guaranteed if he would be patient and agree to Saturday, August 25th.

He was in agreement.

It was then it hit me. I was going to Calgary to face John Melvin Hill on camera for all friends, family and colleagues to see. All I could think about was placing my hands around his neck and pulling his throat out. All I could feel was fear and loathing,

Marty called me during the evening on Wednesday, August 22nd to tell me where the Lad worked. He had re-invented himself, this time as a so-called Kitchen Manager/Chef for a restaurant called Broken City. I was very appreciative and passed this information along to Robert.

Meanwhile, the Lad had called Shelagh Conroy to tell her that if she wanted a preview of what to expect from him, she was to tune into Calgary's Breakfast Television on Friday morning.

This was unbelievable. Seldom does the person of interest to a program like W-Five confirm his whereabouts and confirm an aspect of his fraudulent ways on television, hours before the arrival of the W-Five crew.

He was a "chef." This was hysterical. He has managed to gain employment without credentials and

Perfect Prey

The Last Supper

As if by fate, I had booked an evening with my dear friends the Marshalls for Friday, August 24th, at their home. We made this plan in July. I had no idea how important this evening would be as a way to ease me toward one of the toughest moments in my life. I have known this couple, indeed their family, for well over a decade and have loved every minute.

This evening was special. Mr. Date.Ca was being launched into my social world. He was meeting the people I love and observing the traits I value. I thought this made us a couple.

Mr. Date.Ca excused himself from the table for a few moments allowing Val and Paul to ask me: "Was there anything you don't want him to know about you?" I think this question was in reference to the con artist incident. I am still laughing.

I excused myself from the table to visit the washroom and on return was detained by a cell phone call. This call was very important. It was from David, a long time friend who had suffered the loss of his wife back in June. It was my promise to David to spend time with him following the summer. Receiving his call on the eve of my potential vindication or demise reminded me of my life back on earth. His experience was so much more significant than any of the nonsense I was about to endure. Nevertheless, I had work to do and knew that whatever the outcome, it would make for one heck of a dinner conversation between friends.

Morning came and I was reminded that evil walks among us. I was hours away from flying directly to the most evil person I had ever encountered. Yes, even more evil than Lawzilla. I am scared. I am leaving behind the love of my family and heading directly into the arms of a predator. Please God let this decision be the right one.

So here I sit in Row 23, Seat C enjoying a glass of chardonnay. The Pilot tells us that we are within two hours of our destination. I would prefer to be two years. Once on the ground in Calgary I will be supported by the crew from W-Five. They are all wonderful people with important jobs but I have no illusions about their loyalty. I am the story; an episodic blip on their production schedule.

The plane is about to land and I am exhausted. It is 11:40 P.M. in my body clock and I have been awake since June 14, 2005. I just want to collect my suitcase, hail a cab and slip under the covers. On check-in, I am asked to call Robert. I expected that. I did not expect what I heard.

The date between Shelagh Conroy and the Irish Lad at a local Starbucks went like clockwork. Audio and visual surveillance combined capture the Lad in all his revolting glory.

The predictable rant delivered by the Lad had the crew in hysterics. It was all they could do to sit still and not give their whereabouts away.

Perfect Prey

While Shelagh clutched her coffee cup and likely bit her tongue to prevent laughter, she endured the following storyline from the Lad:

- A life of military service in the Royal Marines fighting in the Falkland Islands
- Tour of duty with Microsoft
- Degree in electrical engineering; a Masters degree in applied math
- A father with countless auto dealerships
- A grandfather and former investment banker
- Coping with the challenges of having a lesbian Mother
- And he was basking in the pride that comes with having a daughter, who is not only a paediatric oncology residence at Children's Hospital, but a hopeless fanatic about Manolo Blanc shoes. To the Lad's credit she owned 13 pairs.

New material was released: The Irish Lad was also a condom runner as a teen, committed to freeing Irish Catholic youth and his main clients were nuns and priests. And breaking news: He was also a judge on Season One of America's Iron Chef!

Shelagh had to cut the date short, citing a previous commitment to a girlfriend. She suggested they resume this fascinating conversation over lunch or dinner the next day. The Lad hesitated because Sundays were dedicated to his daughter. He would call her.

He did call Shelagh and declined a second date stating he found her to be too ambitious, intense, and lacking in affection. I guess sticking his tongue down her throat in the parking lot didn't count as affection.

Perfect Prey

The Irish Lad's background was all about the hug and kisses. Stunned, she called him back and grovelled for a second chance. Shelagh managed to keep him on the phone for 45 minutes, almost begging for another chance.

Sociopaths are all about control. It is in the exertion of control that they experience orgasm. Of course he would see her again. Only it would be on his terms.

Think again Lad – it would be on W-Five's terms!

W-Five had to take the kill shot. With camera and microphones at the ready they waited for Shelagh to greet the Irish Lad just outside the Sheraton's main front entrance. Before he knew what hit him they pounced and pelted questions at him for 10 minutes.

Nothing was spared. He was accused of battering and robbing women, as well as having committed fraud. Rather than keep his head down, he announced that such behaviours made up for his inadequacies. He went on to say that at no time did he feel his conduct with his victims caused them any harm.

Victor Malarek, Senior Reporter for W-Five was brilliant. Firing off one statement of fact after the other he concluded with the question: "What's a boy from Verdun, Quebec, doing with such a rich Irish accent? Have you ever actually been in Ireland?" Then Victor named elementary and secondary schools – in Verdun – attended by the Lad.

With the help of W-Five, a middle-aged divorced woman with two children and a one-eyed dog out-conned the "artist." The crew of W-Five had served justice.

Perfect Prey

Robert felt a little bad for me. His sense was that I missed the party, and he wanted me to have a fair turn. So he suggested that I dress for business and meet him in the lobby on Sunday for Part Two. The plan was to pay the Lad a visit at the Broken City restaurant on 11th Avenue SW.

We arrived at the location by 10:30 A.M., allowing time for us to settle into our base position and to get me wired for sound. I was given my marching orders and they were to approach the bar area and ask for the Irish Lad. If he was in the kitchen, then the plan was to have a staff person tell him that Liz Cole wanted to speak with him.

Once in his fac,e I was to ask him one question. "Why did you lie to my children?"

Meanwhile, Robert would be seated in a booth with a mini-cam and sound man Michael would be outside picking up the feed.

In fairness, none of us expected him to turn up to work today given the beating he took from the crew the night before. However we had to try.

Imagine sitting in a surveillance van, anticipating a run-in with the man who promised marriage. Now look out the car window with me and note the fact that the majority of retail stores were bridal shops.

One shop stood apart from the rest. It was a jewellery shop named Peridot. My birthstone is the peridot and the necklace given to me by Mr. Date.Ca was a string of miniature pearls spotted with peridots. I was wearing this necklace for good luck. It gave me hope in the face of confronting a monster who had served time for brutally assaulting women.

I made my way to the restaurant and focused on nothing other than finding a member of the staff to let the Lad know I was in the house. He was not scheduled to work, but was in the habit of dropping in. Rather than linger, I left the Broken City and made my way back to the SUV. Robert and Michael followed.

I suggested to Robert that we contact Marty to see if he could gain information about which residence the Lad was occupying courtesy of Jewish Community Services. He made the call and left a message.

The new plan was to give the Lad a chance to tell his side of the story in a calm and controlled setting such as the hotel. The element of surprise would be the arrival of a "mystery date." I sat and waited in my hotel room for Robert to confirm this arrangement.

At 4:20 P.M. I got the call. Robert has communicated with the Irish Lad and pitched the offer. The Lad was completely devastated by the attack from W-Five and wanted details. Ironically, he wants to know who, what, where, why and when. Robert was clear about the fact that this show will air. The Lad bemoans that this broadcast will ruin his life.

Karma. JUSTICE!

Robert offers the Verdun Quebec Lad the chance to state his side of the story. He gave the Lad the chance to think about it and would call him back.

hope in the face of confronting a monster who had served time for brutally assaulting women.

I made my way to the restaurant and focused on nothing other than finding a member of the staff to let the Lad know I was in the house. He was not scheduled to work, but was in the habit of dropping in. Rather than linger, I left the Broken City and made my way back to the SUV. Robert and Michael followed.

I suggested to Robert that we contact Marty to see if he could gain information about which residence the Lad was occupying courtesy of Jewish Community Services. He made the call and left a message.

The new plan was to give the Lad a chance to tell his side of the story in a calm and controlled setting such as the hotel. The element of surprise would be the arrival of a "mystery date." I sat and waited in my hotel room for Robert to confirm this arrangement.

At 4:20 P.M. I got the call. Robert has communicated with the Irish Lad and pitched the offer. The Lad was completely devastated by the attack from W-Five and wanted details. Ironically, he wants to know who, what, where, why and when. Robert was clear about the fact that this show will air. The Lad bemoans that this broadcast will ruin his life.

Karma. JUSTICE!

Robert offers the Verdun Quebec Lad the chance to state his side of the story. He gave the Lad the chance to think about it and would call him back.

Perfect Prey

Robert felt a little bad for me. His sense was that I missed the party, and he wanted me to have a fair turn. So he suggested that I dress for business and meet him in the lobby on Sunday for Part Two. The plan was to pay the Lad a visit at the Broken City restaurant on 11th Avenue SW.

We arrived at the location by 10:30 A.M., allowing time for us to settle into our base position and to get me wired for sound. I was given my marching orders and they were to approach the bar area and ask for the Irish Lad. If he was in the kitchen, then the plan was to have a staff person tell him that Liz Cole wanted to speak with him.

Once in his fac,e I was to ask him one question. "Why did you lie to my children?"

Meanwhile, Robert would be seated in a booth with a mini-cam and sound man Michael would be outside picking up the feed.

In fairness, none of us expected him to turn up to work today given the beating he took from the crew the night before. However we had to try.

Imagine sitting in a surveillance van, anticipating a run-in with the man who promised marriage. Now look out the car window with me and note the fact that the majority of retail stores were bridal shops.

One shop stood apart from the rest. It was a jewellery shop named Peridot. My birthstone is the peridot and the necklace given to me by Mr. Date.Ca was a string of miniature pearls spotted with peridots. I was wearing this necklace for good luck. It gave me

Perfect Prey

Robert did in fact call him back and rescinded the offer. They had what they came for and it was done.

My work was done in Calgary. I was tired, wired and wanted to go home. I wanted to fly into Toronto Pearson airport and greet my baby, Rachel, on her return flight from California visiting with her Father.

I wonder if Daddy packed her bag with child support cheques.

Robert invited me to join the crew for dinner and I accepted. I had the extraordinary pleasure of dining with Shelagh Conroy; who is exceptionally intelligent, gritty as hell, and capable of great tenderness. Though our time at dinner was brief we parted ways with hugs and kisses; mindful of the fact that we traveled into the Lad's dark world as a team.

I crawled into bed knowing that my 5:30 A.M. wake-up call would launch me back to the people and places where I feel most safe. There will be too few moments for my imagination to work overtime.

Why? I have less than 48 hours to prepare for our move away from Mom's house to our first home as Mother and Daughters. I have assumed a calming mantra about the apartment making it possible to manage days of heavy lifting. "Three bedrooms, two bathrooms, three bedrooms, two bathrooms." It takes so little to make me smile.

Sitting at Pearson International Airport waiting for Rachel to arrive, I am delighted to receive a call from Sarah who is also at Terminal One. There is time for a hug and a drink. Sarah's wit is, as always, spot on. I told her that the Lad's fictitious daughter, Siobhan, is now a paediatric oncologocial resident at Calgary's Children's Hospital. Without flinching she quickly remarked, "I guess she works with Doctors without Borders."

It's 4:30 P.M. and Rachel has landed. My fatigue is undeniable. My tears are choking me. Just then, I receive a call from Mr. Date.Ca and his voice manages to calm me and create anxiety all at the same time. I know that the days ahead are insanely busy with our residential move coupled by his son's departure for university. Mindful of the time, I cut to the chase and ask: "When will I see you?" He rattles off a list of commitments, and I become detached from the call. Too tired to manage this information, I suggest we talk later in the evening.

My blonde beauty appeared through the gate doors, and I pounced on her with the strength of a mother bear. We find our way to the airport limo. Once comfortably seated, she began to "debrief" me about her less than stellar experience in California.

At home, during dinner I began to unfold the details of my experiences in Calgary. Mom, Tess and Rachel listened attentively. Then out from the silence came the words: "Mom you are both smart and brave." Tess had honoured me. My choices were the right ones, and I had served my daughters' best interests.

The beauty of Tess's remarks had to be tabled for another day. She needed a drive to a friend's house. A knock came to the door and it was a friend of Rachel's who missed her terribly and wanted to get the giggle-and-squeal fest started. With everyone's needs under control, I made my way down the street to Michelle and Andrew, for a glass of wine and storytelling.

I remembered that I had promised to call Mr. Date.Ca to share the story and make plans to get together. I called Mr. Date Ca. We agreed to meet for lunch.

Exhausted I made my way to the restaurant for noon. It was bittersweet. I wanted to be with him and I knew he did not agree with the events that had transpired. There is always so much tension between us. Our lives are complicated by bad separations and divorce; our geography always challenging; our children ever changing and worthy of our time and energy and our finances completely decimated by our spouses. I prayed that two negatives would make a positive, but I feared otherwise.

November 1, 2007

I went to dinner at Mr. Date.Ca's house and it started off as all the other dates had, with hugs, great kissing, wine and cheeky banter. We cooked dinner, sat down and ate and then all hell broke loose. Actually, I broke loose. I stepped outside the boundaries of polite conversation and let him have it. I was tired of everything. That's what happens when you fail to be honest. I ranted on about his failure to take more deliberate action concerning his personal affairs. I knew that this was none of my business. I freaked out at him in the process.

The doormat was weaving herself back together. The anger I felt, for not asking the simplest questions when I had the chance back in August during our car ride home from Collingwood, would not stay down. I did not ask him one simple question back then which was: "How is it possible that you lived with your wife and communicated divorced status to me? From there the floodgates opened in my mind and the questions were choking me. "Why haven't I been introduced to your 14 year old son?" Why haven't I met at least one of your friends or family members?"

As if I needed more reason to become unglued, I talked about how the W-Five episode was airing on November 3rd. I had reason to be cautious, as the man I hunted down is dangerous. I had every right to be nervous about how the show would appear to the outside world.

In response, Mr. Date.Ca reminded me that he was against the whole thing from the beginning. I had heard that recording once too often. It boiled down to the fact that he was the only one that actually wasn't supportive of my conviction to right a serious wrong. It mattered that he was not in my corner no matter what. I was in the presence of a stranger.

Worse, I was only casual dating. It was nothing significant; nothing that mattered. I was his cheerleader.

I am born to the role of cheerleader, but have tasted the thrill of the game as a player since revealing the truth about the Irish Lad to the nation. In the face of a losing game with my ex-Husband, I managed to rally the strength to take one more shot, everyday, for the sake of my children. I can't give my energy away to anything or anyone that does not respect my courage or fuel my resolve.

Saturday, November 3, 2007

A long day awaited me and everyone in my corner. The beauty of being an impoverished single Mom is that you cannot distract yourself with shopping for needless things such as warm winter clothing or comfortable shoes. Instead you clean, and, in my case, bake as well.

Mom's house was broadcast central, and I was looking forward to being in the company of Auntie Peggy, Kerry Watt, Mom, Rachel and her girlfriends Jen, and Gen. I was also invited to join Michelle and Andrew at their home for a post-show drink. Tess had arranged a last minute gathering back at the apartment for her chums to view and chew on pizza.

Lloyd Robertson was on deck setting the stage for the viewing audience. I sat in a self-hugging position that managed to incorporate a big glass of wine. I have always been flexible.

In a matter of 15 minutes, my portion of the Risky Business: Cyber Shark episode was over. I was intact and smiling. W-Five had masterfully edited the story, leaving the audience with a natural hatred for the Lad and the opinion that I was a reasonable and articulate woman. My prayer was that viewers would conclude that if this could happen to me, it could happen to anyone. I am confident that this message came through loud and clear.

My cell phone rang. It was David. His words were simple. They conveyed his pride about my actions. This beautiful man, my friend, had stayed in to watch the horror of my life unfold on television and found the words to make me feel powerful.

I made my way down the street to Andrew and Michelle's house for drinks and debriefing. I also managed to tell them about David's call, and they asked me if there was more to this friendship than I had let on. There was not. We were just friends.

With the W-Five story now part of the public domain, I have the Canadian Living article to look forward to, and maybe interest to publish my book. I have no idea what to expect. I do know that I will sleep tonight.

My cell phone rang. It was David. His words were simple. They conveyed his pride about my actions. This beautiful man, my friend, had stayed in to watch the horror of my life unfold on television and found the words to make me feel powerful.

I made my way down the street to Andrew and Michelle's house for drinks and debriefing. I also managed to tell them about David's call, and they asked me if there was more to this friendship than I had let on. There was not. We were just friends.

With the W-Five story now part of the public domain, I have the Canadian Living article to look forward to, and maybe interest to publish my book. I have no idea what to expect. I do know that I will sleep tonight.

my children. I can't give my energy away to anything or anyone that does not respect my courage or fuel my resolve.

Saturday, November 3, 2007

A long day awaited me and everyone in my corner. The beauty of being an impoverished single Mom is that you cannot distract yourself with shopping for needless things such as warm winter clothing or comfortable shoes. Instead you clean, and, in my case, bake as well.

Mom's house was broadcast central, and I was looking forward to being in the company of Auntie Peggy, Kerry Watt, Mom, Rachel and her girlfriends Jen, and Gen. I was also invited to join Michelle and Andrew at their home for a post-show drink. Tess had arranged a last minute gathering back at the apartment for her chums to view and chew on pizza.

Lloyd Robertson was on deck setting the stage for the viewing audience. I sat in a self-hugging position that managed to incorporate a big glass of wine. I have always been flexible.

In a matter of 15 minutes, my portion of the Risky Business: Cyber Shark episode was over. I was intact and smiling. W-Five had masterfully edited the story, leaving the audience with a natural hatred for the Lad and the opinion that I was a reasonable and articulate woman. My prayer was that viewers would conclude that if this could happen to me, it could happen to anyone. I am confident that this message came through loud and clear.

Perfect Prey

Monday, November 5, 2007

I gave thanks today. Robert, Chad and the crew, including Victor Malarek, created a wrinkle in time for this weary traveler and changed my life. I could not have found my way back to feeling good about myself without their participation.

Robert responded to my note with a surprise. A viewer, Mandy, responded to the program indicating that she had been victimized by John Hill and was hoping to communicate with the "woman" on the show. I despair for any victim that comes forward but vow to keep them near my heart and will do anything to assist them to find the peace of mind that for me was stolen as a result of his treachery.

I made contact with Mandy right away. My first responsibility was to assure her of my support and complete acceptance. My second responsibility was to happily welcome her to a new reality: "Together we are unstoppable."

Mandy and I went on to exchange very difficult communication today. With her permission and name changed, I will share her story. I fear this is only the tip if the iceberg.

Mandy's Story (as told directly by e-mail):

(Please note that I'm 30 years old...and not all that naïve...this guy was smooth)

I understand how busy you are and will explain my situation briefly to you and if I can help in anyway, please let me know.

I put an ad on Craigslist a few weeks before the last Calgary Stampede asking for any serving jobs over Stampede to boost my funds for a very short trip to France with my girlfriend that was supposed to happen in October. I realize this put me in a vulnerable position, but I was desperate and knew I could make the extra money.

John Hill (this is the man I recognized off TV, and the name I was given) was persistent on pushing across a very wealthy, powerful image when he responded to my ad. When we met, he was working at the Whiskey helping a friend, but stated he is usually traveling the world (embellished about his private plane and house in France, his one daughter who is a surgeon, his 'high society' lifestyle, his worldliness, languages, etc.)

After a week of falling for his whirlwind of seduction and lies, he suggested to me that if I were his girlfriend, he would fly me to France himself but not to do any 'servant jobs' again.

During Stampede I can usually make about $5,000 to $8,000 in the course of those 10 days. I didn't work at all because he had told me he was going to fly me there. After the last day of Stampede, I never saw him *again; phone # disconnected. I tried to push my Europe dream out of my head, but one thing I couldn't forget, however, is how the last time we were intimate, he had tried to get me pregnant saying how much he wants to marry me, etc.*

He destroyed my dreams of making money to experience Europe for his own selfish sexual game. I ended up being pregnant after all; I had the abortion just over a month ago.

I hate this man, Liz. I really do. I hate myself for being so lonely that I could actually let something evil like this into my life. He didn't con any money out of me, but certainly conned my opportunity for experience because he made me trust him with such extent and now I'm SO gun-shy about meeting men over the Internet...with my full time work, school and family schedule, that was the only way I had to meet a nice guy.

Regardless, I must sound like an idiot and I'm sure you think I am; I've never told anyone about this except for you. I guess when you have nothing and someone shows you the world, you want to embrace if full force and believe every word is true. I guess this is how we learn.

This man is deeply disturbed, and I am SO SORRY for what happened to you. I really am. You are an amazing person. If there is a group formed or anything of the like, I would like to be a part and YES, TOGETHER WE ARE UNSTOPPABLE.

- *Mandy*

John Melvin Hill remains at large. His most recent employment was for a restaurant called the Short Game in Calgary. My understanding is that he resigned on November 3rd in anticipation of the reaction that awaited him by his employer, colleagues, and restaurant patrons.

Back in Toronto, collection notices from Bell Canada gather as well as a pawn ticket notice from Oliver's Jewellers for redemption. Mr. Hill hocked an expensive watch not likely belonging to him.

My hope is that a victim or victims who have seen the broadcast will recognize him and be in a position to issue outstanding warrants for his arrest. It is only a matter of time before his actions escalate and the authorities are able to respond.

Part 4

That was then and this is now

In my search for the Irish Lad, I came across a brilliant website called www.lovefraud.com. It was like walking into a room where everyone could honestly say: "Been there, done that." Being victimized often results in loss of dignity and lays the groundwork for social isolation. Even the more brazen among us walk through the paces. We may appear socially active, but we battle our self-worth most of the time.

As a survivor of romantic fraud I know how desperate you can become in your search to find level ground. I knew that my mental health would have reached a place of no return had I not taken up the fight to find the Lad and regain my dignity. My courage and conviction created a way out of the dark. My actions were deliberate, organized and time-sensitive. I was able to experience results from the choices I made.

This is very serious. It has redefined how I measure my own success. It would be an understatement to say that life doesn't always work the way we like it to. In fact, the business of living well requires us to dispense with the notion that other people, places, and things will devote themselves to making us happy.

Perfect Prey

In order to remain a successful person, I have accepted difficulties as challenges, rolled up my sleeves and worked through them. I have learned to accept without exception that being successful does not mean escaping unfairness.

I recognize that I fell into the trap of allowing my conditions, not my decisions to define me. Knowing this, and acting on it, are two different things. I am surrounded by conditions that are abstract and therefore, frustrating as hell. Concepts like fairness, justice, integrity, honesty, and morality are among the abstract conditions that drive me to distraction.

I would rather face concrete conditions that can be touched, tasted, observed and heard. I would rather my ex-Husband and men like the Irish Lad hit me so hard that I am knocked to the ground. That probably sounds ridiculous, but I know that I would recover because such cruelties can be measured and responded to in a finite way.

So many of us have whispered the words: "God grant me the serenity to accept the things I cannot change, the courage to change the things I can, and the wisdom to know the difference." These are powerful words and if truly endorsed, will guide any one of us toward personal success. On a good day where abstract conditions have not paralyzed my purpose, I am able to know the difference between existing and living.

It is my intention to raise your eyebrows sufficiently in order to reduce your risk for becoming someone's prey. There are tremendous resources that profile sociopath predators, who con and scam the innocent. Vancouver-based Dr. Robert Hare is the foremost expert on sociopaths and psychopathic behaviour and I strongly recommend that your own search for truth begins with his body of work.

I am already stigmatized by the misguided opinions of well meaning individuals who can't understand how a seemingly clever gal like me could be taken in. The comments I receive are not intended to be cruel, but they do hurt. My appearance on W-Five conveyed the real me. I am articulate, reasonable, and infinitely trusting.

I am also aware of my vulnerabilities. It is what I do with this awareness that reduces my risk for future manipulation. The wisdom of law enforcement and mental health professionals would have me believe that if my feet were firmly planted on the ground, I would have been less likely a target. My own experience tells me that the only thing that keeps my feet firmly planted on the ground is when I have gum on the soles of my shoes.

Getting inside my own head scares me to death. It forces me to say – indeed scream – that my need for approval by others is so strong that I often do too much for other people, or even let myself be used so that I won't be rejected for other reasons. I believed that being nice – a four-letter word – would reduce my chances of being left behind and receiving hurtful, even dangerous treatment from others.

The simple act of giving the power of "nice" front of the line access to relationships has served as a wake-up call. My actions have created significant emotional events that demand I hit the brakes, pull over to the side of the road and give my head a shake.

With every significant emotional event comes the opportunity for learning and ultimately acting on that learning by doing things differently. When I say differently, I mean by being fully present, mindful and alert. Otherwise, you are at risk of remaining in reaction mode, which places you at increased risk for being the victim of other people's actions.

This simple awareness allowed me to face my shadows and give rise to new ways of seeing the world around me. It's quite amazing what can happen when you pull back the curtain and let a little light in. It's even more amazing what can happen when you step into that light and do at least one thing differently.

The beauty of self-awareness is that it may remain under construction for your entire life, and because I am in no hurry to have all the answers, I must necessarily downgrade my wisdom to 'Lizdom' for it to be of any benefit to you. Only when my actions result in constructive change will I acknowledge my potential for being considered a wise person. For now, I have to settle for being a wise ass.

Lizdom One:

There is a great saying that says the challenge of breathing is to keep doing it. I get that. The problem is that I had begun to regard dating as nature's other life force. When you combine that behaviour with the price of being too nice, you soon realize that dating without a net can result in exploitation. Even when I realized that I was being manipulated, used, and taken advantage of, my self-imposed, nice-for-life program prevented me from communicating anger, frustration, and limits. Behind the scenes, there existed a level of drama that relayed nagging doubts, painful insecurities, and unresolved fears that arose from a failed marriage.

My game face coupled with my sense of humour combined to prevent me from telling myself and the people I loved that I was very unhappy, furious, tormented, and so disappointed with how my life had played out that it just became easier to fake life rather than attempt to fix it.

Divorce is a painful reminder that effort does not always equal love and appreciation.

The Ontario Family Court system confirmed that being nice had nothing to do with being at risk of receiving unkind treatment.

Lizdom Two:

A disappointing marriage and a perilous dating relationship taught me that compromising my own values, needs, and identity cost way too much. Had I said what was on my mind, even risked communicating "un-nice" feelings, I could have reduced my experience with depression and protected my children from unrelenting cruelty and disrespect. Yes, both in my marriage and in dating a sociopath.

Lizdom Three:

It is entirely possible to care about others and to look after yourself in mind, body, and spirit. I failed to see myself as being able to act from enlightened self-interest. I could only see myself as acting, period. I performed the role of the selfless single Mom. Enslavement was familiar to me, and I stopped seeing the punitive behaviour of others in favour of ramping up my own people-pleasing skill set.

I have love in my life. Love teaches me that if I continue to fail to communicate my needs then I will continue to experience trouble and disappointment. It is also realistic to expect the people you love to help you fulfill your needs and even exceed your expectations.

Lizdom Four:

My romantic relationships have taught me that any man who feels threatened or diminished by my essential self, successes, and even failures, is not worth the effort and I should look elsewhere. You may wonder why I even continue to look at all. To this I must reply, love. In the grand lobby of life, I have decided to check in at reception desk, rather than hide behind a visitor's badge.

I was manipulated by a sociopath, not a garden variety liar. In a strange way that truth allows for hope and healing. There can be love in my future because my encounter with darkness had a beginning, middle and end. In some ways I was fortunate. My days are not strung together with lies, misinformation and errors of omission as they once were in my marriage, or, by comparison, a much more cruel and debilitating experience that resulted in my becoming a target for a sociopath and the victim of romantic fraud.

We all lie. We are not all afflicted with an anti-social personality disorder. For most of us encountering a liar is as bad as it's going to get. Just recognizing the body language, tonality, and words used by a liar may be enough to spare you the indignity of being manipulated, humiliated, or disappointed.

The practice of lying is rooted in our evolution. For the most part, we begin to lie as young children mostly because we sense that the truth may result in greater personal consequence. For instance, it is easier to say you completed your homework rather than enlist the speech-making skills of your parents as they drill home the importance of having upstanding personal organizational skills.

Lizdom Five:

I have learned that the act of lying is easily detected if the liar is neither pathological, nor a sociopath. By comparing the body language, tonality and word choices used by liars and sociopaths, you will have a few tools of awareness at your disposal. However, this information comes with the warning that the mind will only perceive what it wants to. My encounter with a sociopath taught me that the use of his lies is nothing short of being among the tools of his trade.

Lies and body language:

Liars will keep a safe distance from their victim and will always be mindful of the nearest exit. Sociopaths do not require an escape hatch.

Liars may slouch, or reduce the physical size of their body by crossing their legs and arms. Sociopaths will stand tall, with arms wide open suggesting there is nothing they cannot withstand.

Liars often make use of a distancing object such as a pillow, chair, table, door, or window to physically mark the space between their story and the truth. Sociopaths do not need any physical dividers because they have an arsenal of lies at their disposal.

Lies and use of voice tone and timing:

Liars may have the lead-in lie up and ready to go, but typically struggle with follow-up, or substantiating lesser lies. The liar will want to get in and get out. Sociopaths are not conscious of time. Lying and talking are one in the same.

Liars may use a flat tone, or apply an unusual amount of volume to cover up a flawed storyline. Sociopaths will use intonation, animation and hand puppets if necessary!

Liars may use time to draw out their story to such an extent that you have become sidetracked and easily confused. Sociopaths use this technique effortlessly as if to beat you into submission.

Lies and word selection:

Liars select words to protect their own interests. Sociopaths select words that ae meant to cause harm to others.

Liars know the power of keeping their word quantity short, simple, and to the point. Sociopaths delight in using a combination of word quality and quantity.

Liars may appear to say one thing, but mean another. Sociopaths are emphatic about their message, or so casually cool that you can't gauge the integrity of the message.

The practice of lying is rooted in our evolution. For the most part, we begin to lie as young children mostly because we sense that the truth may result in greater personal consequence. For instance, it is easier to say you completed your homework rather than enlist the speech-making skills of your parents as they drill home the importance of having upstanding personal organizational skills.

Lizdom Five:

I have learned that the act of lying is easily detected if the liar is neither pathological, nor a sociopath. By comparing the body language, tonality and word choices used by liars and sociopaths, you will have a few tools of awareness at your disposal. However, this information comes with the warning that the mind will only perceive what it wants to. My encounter with a sociopath taught me that the use of his lies is nothing short of being among the tools of his trade.

Lies and body language:

Liars will keep a safe distance from their victim and will always be mindful of the nearest exit. Sociopaths do not require an escape hatch.

Liars may slouch, or reduce the physical size of their body by crossing their legs and arms. Sociopaths will stand tall, with arms wide open suggesting there is nothing they cannot withstand.

Liars often make use of a distancing object such as a pillow, chair, table, door, or window to physically mark the space between their story and the truth. Sociopaths do not need any physical dividers because they have an arsenal of lies at their disposal.

Lies and use of voice tone and timing:

Liars may have the lead-in lie up and ready to go, but typically struggle with follow-up, or substantiating lesser lies. The liar will want to get in and get out. Sociopaths are not conscious of time. Lying and talking are one in the same.

Liars may use a flat tone, or apply an unusual amount of volume to cover up a flawed storyline. Sociopaths will use intonation, animation and hand puppets if necessary!

Liars may use time to draw out their story to such an extent that you have become sidetracked and easily confused. Sociopaths use this technique effortlessly as if to beat you into submission.

Lies and word selection:

Liars select words to protect their own interests. Sociopaths select words that ae meant to cause harm to others.

Liars know the power of keeping their word quantity short, simple, and to the point. Sociopaths delight in using a combination of word quality and quantity.

Liars may appear to say one thing, but mean another. Sociopaths are emphatic about their message, or so casually cool that you can't gauge the integrity of the message.

Lizdom Six:

It always amazes me how relaxed a liar becomes once the lie has been "successfully" delivered. Not funny, but reassuring in that you can recognize a glimmer of remorse in the liar. Another familiar phrase frequently used by a liar is "to tell you the truth," or "to be perfectly honest," as if to suggest the alternative is an option. Liars will also toss in a few facts to give their message some teeth.

By contrast and direct experience, a sociopath never relaxes after spinning his yarn because he does not connect being dishonest with lack of remorse. You will recall from my journal notes that the Irish Lad overwhelmed me with details, so-called facts, and too much information, making the most absurd stories believable by virtue of how unbelievable they seemed.

Still, many of you want to know one thing: How much money did that bastard get? Everyone wants to know how much money the Lad was able to con from my wallet. This is all too common an assumption about the intentions of a con artist.

Recall if you will Mandy's story. We value money as the single most important commodity. It is money, or material wealth that is of interest to the law. It is the size of the heist that gives con artists their notoriety. But the greater commodities are time, trust and dreams.

The Irish Lad abused my time. When you are a self-employed, single mother working seven days a week all the while navigating the Ontario Family Court system for child support, time is everything. It is time that allows us to set goals and take action. It is in time that we measure the moments with our loved ones. It is in time that we are able to earn money. That makes his involvement in our life sinister, manipulative, and cruel beyond comparison. Money is like a rubber ball that will bounce back. Family, friends, spirit, and health are made of crystal and if dropped, may shatter with little hope of remaining intact.

Lizdom Seven:

Spend your time wisely. Surround yourself with people, activities, commitments, and moments that combine to create a life story you would wish on anyone.

The Irish Lad abused my trust. Healthy relationships prosper when two parties are able to communicate clear, open and honest messages about one's self and others. While some of us are naturally guarded, meaning we operate in a lower-risk comfort zone, I have always been Liz unplugged with respect to trust. I am not an infant or a moron. I am instinctively trusting in the same way that I am tall and have brown eyes.

My mistake was to give away my trust without first building a foundation for its fair and appropriate exchange. Despite a failed marriage, followed by less than successful dating experiences, I failed to catch my breath and examine the circumstances that surrounded me. I needed to learn to regard trust as a gift two people share. This gift does not need to be grand, rather, small, personal, and supported by a full return policy.

The Irish Lad worked diligently to create a trusting environment in our early weeks together by following through on his promises. His words matched his actions for a short time, which made it possible for me to readily give him the gift of my trust. However, when his actions later failed to reflect his promises, I flicked the switch to autopilot and continued to trust him as if I was sleepwalking.

The Lad also had a running advantage in that he knew that my court battles represented the ultimate act of betrayal. By comparison, his missteps would pale against the actions of a spouse and father, who neglected his responsibilities.

Lizdom Eight:

It is only with the passage of time and experience that you can truly process the awesome benefits of a trusting relationship. Think of your relationships as climbing a ladder together. Ascending each rung is the result of mutual confidence. Granted, where one party might be more naturally trusting, the other may need to extend his or her hand and be encouraged to step ever so slightly out of his or her comfort zone in order to rise to the next level.

The Irish Lad abused my dreams. This is a tricky one for a person who comes from modest means and who lost everything due to a difficult divorce. While the trappings of material wealth capture most peoples' attention, including my own and that of my children, and Mother, I must say that my dream was sinister, dishonest, and loaded with the bittersweet taste of revenge.

Don't misread my preoccupation with the commodity of time as not recognizing the pain of any victim who has experienced material loss. I despair for any victim of a sociopath. I know that being taken for money or material wealth is horrible. I speak only from my vantage point which is through the eyes of my family. I can't recapture the time lost as a result of the Lad's abuse.

Lizdom Nine:

My own experience has taught me that the most powerful tool available to victims like, Marty, Darlene, Mandy. and me, is our voice. Silence serves the sociopath and helps create an ever-expanding arena where he can play his game. By linking our messages we create an increasingly small world and hopefully will attract the attention of law enforcement.

The business world also needs to step up and implement the critical steps associated with both the hiring process and protecting their customers. Darlene was completely and utterly victimized by John Hill and Ford Leasing. It is amazing to me that a company that prides itself on providing a household name brand would lease a vehicle without performing any kind of credit check and then hold the law-abiding citizen-victim accountable for the con artist's fraud.

All Darlene wanted was to have John Hill's name removed from the lease agreement in order to sell the tainted vehicle back to the dealership. Instead, she was told that his rights pervaded, and she would need his compliance in the form a signature by Hill on a release form. Call me crazy, but I don't see this man agreeing to sign his name to anything. Ford Leasing knows all about his criminal history and has proof of his fraudulent ways as shown on W-Five. But unless things have recently changed, paperwork and an unyielding process prevail at Ford. By the way, how is the North American automobile industry performing these days?

John Melvin Hill is a repeat offender who continues to exploit victims, employers, the marketplace, and the justice system. He abuses our time, steals our money and damages the mental health of his victims. He may fall under the radar of the law, but he has not fallen under the radar of our nation, thanks to W-Five and readers like you.

Parting Lizdoms:

This is what I experienced:

I have spent the last two and a half years taking risks without considering the possible consequences of my actions. My challenges, opportunities, and fears, had shoved me so far outside my comfort zone that I had little or no time to dwell on any potential costs, losses, discomforts or pain.

Writing this story down has allowed me to relive the experiences of the past several years, and has taught me to take responsibility for my actions. I have now come to acknowledge myself as a courageous person.

This is how I feel:

I feel ashamed that I allowed myself to believe that my life's work could be delegated to someone else, even if only momentarily. I have no one but myself to blame for selling myself short. Wanting to live happily ever after is one thing, but I failing to do the work and opting to take a shortcut is another. I feel rage for the harm brought upon my children.

Friends, family, and workmates continue to rally behind the way I managed this personal fiasco. They catch me when I fall down hard upon myself. They are swift to remind me that I "did the right thing by bringing my story to the public."

This is only partially comforting because I know that if I had done the right thing in the first place, meaning clean up my emotional house, I would not have been as vulnerable to the tactics of John Hill. Note: I do not fully suggest that I could have avoided being the victim of romantic fraud. It is that small point that allows me to give myself a break from the daily self-loathing sessions I inflict upon myself.

This is what I know:

We teach people how to treat us. Our tone of voice, words, body language, values, and temperament send clues to others that they in turn gather and act on.

This simple truth combined with having the good sense to be selective about who we want to spend our time with, work for and ultimately, share love with is all that really matters. Time flies when you are in the moment of being with people who fill your heart and mind. Yet, many of us muddle through unfixable relationships because we have forgotten how to feel at ease with ourselves and with others. In my own case, being with myself presented the greater discomfort. I have always managed to rise to the occasion of being among other people. The further I can get away from being inside my own head the better. This is changing process prevail at Ford. By the way, how is the North American automobile industry performing these days?

John Melvin Hill is a repeat offender who continues to exploit victims, employers, the marketplace, and the justice system. He abuses our time, steals our money and damages the mental health of his victims. He may fall under the radar of the law, but he has not fallen under the radar of our nation, thanks to W-Five and readers like you.

Parting Lizdoms:

This is what I experienced:

I have spent the last two and a half years taking risks without considering the possible consequences of my actions. My challenges, opportunities, and fears, had shoved me so far outside my comfort zone that I had little or no time to dwell on any potential costs, losses, discomforts or pain.

Writing this story down has allowed me to relive the experiences of the past several years, and has taught me to take responsibility for my actions. I have now come to acknowledge myself as a courageous person.

This is how I feel:

I feel ashamed that I allowed myself to believe that my life's work could be delegated to someone else, even if only momentarily. I have no one but myself to blame for selling myself short. Wanting to live happily ever after is one thing, but I failing to do the work and opting to take a shortcut is another. I feel rage for the harm brought upon my children.

Friends, family, and workmates continue to rally behind the way I managed this personal fiasco. They catch me when I fall down hard upon myself. They are swift to remind me that I "did the right thing by bringing my story to the public."

This is only partially comforting because I know that if I had done the right thing in the first place, meaning clean up my emotional house, I would not have been as vulnerable to the tactics of John Hill. Note: I do not fully suggest that I could have avoided being the victim of romantic fraud. It is that small point that allows me to give myself a break from the daily self-loathing sessions I inflict upon myself.

This is what I know:

We teach people how to treat us. Our tone of voice, words, body language, values, and temperament send clues to others that they in turn gather and act on.

This simple truth combined with having the good sense to be selective about who we want to spend our time with, work for and ultimately, share love with is all that really matters. Time flies when you are in the moment of being with people who fill your heart and mind. Yet, many of us muddle through unfixable relationships because we have forgotten how to feel at ease with ourselves and with others. In my own case, being with myself presented the greater discomfort. I have always managed to rise to the occasion of being among other people. The further I can get away from being inside my own head the better. This is changing because I am changing and recognize that essentially, I am pretty damn terrific!

This is what I want:

I want to know that it is safe for me to be myself when I am in the presence of other people, particularly men. This will come with time provided I pay attention to what I am feeling about myself and what I want from both myself and others.

I have learned that in order to make my dreams come true, I must first wake up!
The light of day brings with it the chance to do things differently and better. I am blessed to have the strength to tell my story. I am wise to recognize that my strength comes from the love of my family and friends.

I am empowered by the possibility that all I need to do is give myself a little more credit for all that I have accomplished in the past two and a half years. And as such, set out to do what must be done: live well in mind, body, and spirit.

John Hill always told me that the best revenge was living well. What he failed to mention was that in the case of a sociopath with significant developmental shortcomings, he actually meant to say the best revenge is living well off the backs of others.

I think I will stick to my own 'to-do list' and attend to the business of living well, plain and simple.

Appendix

According to Donna Andersen, founder of www.lovefraud.com, a predator's success is contingent on its prey revealing any one of the following vulnerabilities: loneliness, insecurity, trusting nature, successful, aspiring, trustworthy, nurturing, committed, and, terrifyingly, none of the above.

With respect to the last vulnerability listed, Donna Andersen writes: Perhaps you're tough or savvy enough to avoid the pitfalls listed above. Don't think you're immune. All kinds of people have been manipulated by sociopaths – including corrections officers and psychiatrists who know what they are dealing with.

Even "honour among thieves" doesn't apply to sociopaths. Everyone is a target.

A sociopath, otherwise described as Antisocial Personality Disorder, is characterized by a lack of regard for the moral or legal standards in the local culture.

There is a marked inability to get along with others or abide by societal rules. Sociopaths and psychopaths come from all walks of life.

Perfect Prey

The best offense is a good defense, and here are some of the common features that describe the behaviours of a sociopath:

Glibness and Superficial Charm: "Always on" best describes this personality. Never at a loss for ice-breaking comments and a mile-wide smile.

Manipulative and Cunning: They never recognize the rights of others and see their self-serving behaviours as permissible.

They appear to be charming, yet are covertly hostile and domineering, seeing their victim as merely an instrument to be used. They may dominate and humiliate their victims.

Pathological Lying: Has no problem lying coolly and easily, and it is almost impossible for them to be truthful on a consistent basis. Can create, and get caught up in, a complex belief about their powers and abilities.

They can be extremely convincing and even able to pass lie detector tests.

Grandiose Sense of Self: Feels entitled to certain things as being "their right."

Lack of Remorse, Shame or Guilt: A deep seated rage, which is split off and repressed, is at their core. They do not see others around them as people, but only as targets and opportunities. Instead of friends, they have accomplices who end up as victims.

The end always justifies the means, and they let nothing stand in their way.

Shallow Emotions: The demonstration of warmth, joy, love and compassion are tools that are used to serve ulterior motives.

They are easily outraged by insignificant matters while remaining unmoved by what would upset a normal person.

Incapacity for Love: To experience love you must be able to risk losing love.

Need for Stimulation: Often living on the edge and prone to verbal outbursts. Promiscuity, alcohol and drugs, along with gambling are common behaviours that contribute to their reckless disregard for safety.

Callousness/Lack of Empathy: They are unable to empathize with the pain of their victims, having only contempt for others' feelings of distress, while readily taking advantage of them.

Poor Behavioural Controls/Impulsive Nature: Rage and abuse, alternating with small expressions of love and approval, produce an addictive cycle for abuser and abused, as well as creating hopelessness in the victim.

They believe themselves to be all-powerful, all-knowing and entitled to their every wish. They have no sense of personal boundaries, much less concern for the impact on others.

Early Behaviour Problems/Juvenile Delinquency: Usually has a history of behavioural and academic difficulties, yet "gets by" by conning others.

Perfect Prey

They have problems in making and keeping friends; aberrant behaviour such as cruelty to people or animals.

Stealing is also a prevalent marker for this behaviour. The DSM or Diagnostic Manual of Statistical and Mental Disorders regards the age of 15 as a definitive starting point for measuring antisocial behaviour.

Irresponsibility/Unreliability: They are not concerned about wrecking others' lives and dreams. They are oblivious or indifferent to the devastation they cause. They do not accept blame themselves, but will blame others, even for acts they obviously committed.

Promiscuous Sexual Behaviour/Infidelity: Lack of Realistic Life Plan/Parasitic Lifestyle: They tend to move around a lot or make all encompassing promises for the future. They have a poor work ethic, but exploit others effectively.

Criminal or Entrepreneurial Versatility: Changes their image as needed to avoid prosecution, along with their life story.

There is a very helpful page on www.lovefraud.com that helps the reader spot a con by paying attention to a number of "red flags." I encourage you to visit this site to learn more about these "wake up calls," but have listed them on the next page for your immediate consideration and convenience.

Sociopaths/con artists are:

- Fluent in flattery, which often includes high praise coupled with overwhelming personal attention.
- Comfortable name-dropping, volunteering elaborate career resumes and listing credentials.
- Able to build your trust by creating opportunities that demonstrate their reliability in the short term.
- Noted for slipping up on the smaller details and communicating inconsistencies. When confronted about such loose ends, they will turn the table on their victim by accusing them of mistrust.
- Known for using high pressure tactics. Creating a sense of urgency reduces your time to think and make sound decisions.

As you can see, I have relied heavily on this site for support and guidance. I urge you to do the same. Hours of searching the Internet, reading psychological material and speaking with law enforcement have all served to reinforce the validity of this on-line resource.

It is always wise to contact your own local police authority if you suspect you are in the presence of a con artist, or you can contact Phonebusters toll free at 1-888-495-8501.

They have problems in making and keeping friends; aberrant behaviour such as cruelty to people or animals.

Stealing is also a prevalent marker for this behaviour. The DSM or Diagnostic Manual of Statistical and Mental Disorders regards the age of 15 as a definitive starting point for measuring antisocial behaviour.

Irresponsibility/Unreliability: They are not concerned about wrecking others' lives and dreams. They are oblivious or indifferent to the devastation they cause. They do not accept blame themselves, but will blame others, even for acts they obviously committed.

Promiscuous Sexual Behaviour/Infidelity: Lack of Realistic Life Plan/Parasitic Lifestyle: They tend to move around a lot or make all encompassing promises for the future. They have a poor work ethic, but exploit others effectively.

Criminal or Entrepreneurial Versatility: Changes their image as needed to avoid prosecution, along with their life story.

There is a very helpful page on www.lovefraud.com that helps the reader spot a con by paying attention to a number of "red flags." I encourage you to visit this site to learn more about these "wake up calls," but have listed them on the next page for your immediate consideration and convenience.

Sociopaths/con artists are:

- Fluent in flattery, which often includes high praise coupled with overwhelming personal attention.
- Comfortable name-dropping, volunteering elaborate career resumes and listing credentials.
- Able to build your trust by creating opportunities that demonstrate their reliability in the short term.
- Noted for slipping up on the smaller details and communicating inconsistencies. When confronted about such loose ends, they will turn the table on their victim by accusing them of mistrust.
- Known for using high pressure tactics. Creating a sense of urgency reduces your time to think and make sound decisions.

As you can see, I have relied heavily on this site for support and guidance. I urge you to do the same. Hours of searching the Internet, reading psychological material and speaking with law enforcement have all served to reinforce the validity of this on-line resource.

It is always wise to contact your own local police authority if you suspect you are in the presence of a con artist, or you can contact Phonebusters toll free at 1-888-495-8501.

About the Author:

Liz Cole rebounded from her failed marriage and romantic fraud experience and today proudly celebrates a new marriage to a long-time family friend, who brings to the table four grown sons, infinite patience, a passion for gadgets and a heart that reaches beyond her wildest dreams. In turn, she gives him two remarkable daughters, a one-eyed dog, and a mother-in-law who adores him.

The author works for a national non-profit organization and is often humbled by the heroes she serves in her role.

Liz Cole would also like to go on record noting that Mr. $375-Per-Hour would like the reader to assume he is at least 6'2". Since honesty is the best policy, she wants you to know that if integrity was measured in inches, he'd be a giant.

Closing remarks from the author: "I would not have survived without the love of my Mother and the faith of my daughters."

Perfect Prey

Manor House Publishing
www.manor-house.biz 905-648-2193